AMERICAN FOLKLORE, LEGENDS, AND TALL TALES FOR READERS THEATRE

RECENT TITLES IN TEACHER IDEAS PRESS READERS THEATRE SERIES

Born Storytellers: Readers Theatre Celebrates the Lives and Literature of Classic Authors
Ann N. Black

Around the World Through Holidays: Cross Curricular Readers Theatre
Written and Illustrated by Carol Peterson

Wings of Fancy: Using Readers Theatre to Study Fantasy Genre
Joan Garner

Nonfiction Readers Theatre for Beginning Readers
Anthony D. Fredericks

Mother Goose Readers Theatre for Beginning Readers
Anthony D. Fredericks

MORE Frantic Frogs and Other Frankly Fractured Folktales for Readers Theatre
Anthony D. Fredericks

Songs and Rhymes Readers Theatre for Beginning Readers
Anthony D. Fredericks

Readers Theatre for Middle School Boys: Investigating the Strange and Mysterious
Ann N. Black

African Legends, Myths, and Folktales for Readers Theatre
Anthony D. Fredericks

Against All Odds: Readers Theatre for Grades 3-8
Suzanne I. Barchers and Michael Ruscoe

Readers Theatre for African American History
Jeff Sanders and Nancy I. Sanders

Building Fluency with Readers Theatre: Motivational Strategies, Successful Lessons, and Dynamic Scripts to Develop Fluency, Comprehension, Writing, and Vocabulary
Anthony D. Fredericks

AMERICAN FOLKLORE, LEGENDS, AND TALL TALES FOR READERS THEATRE

Anthony D. Fredericks

Readers Theatre

Teacher Ideas Press
An imprint of Libraries Unlimited
Westport, Connecticut • London

Library of Congress Cataloging-in-Publication Data

Fredericks, Anthony D.
   American folklore, legends, and tall tales for Readers theatre / Anthony D. Fredericks.
     p. cm. — (Readers theatre)
  Includes bibliographical references and index.
  ISBN 978-1-59158-734-7 (alk. paper)
  1. Heroes—United States—Juvenile drama. 2. Folklore—United States—Juvenile drama.
3. Legends—United States—Juvenile drama. 4. Tall tales—United States—Juvenile drama.
5. Children's plays, American. 6. Readers' theater. 7. Drama in education. 8. Folklore—
United States—Study and teaching (Elementary)—Activity programs. 9. Legends—United
 States—Study and teaching (Elementary)—Activity programs. 10. Tall tales—United States—
Study and teaching (Elementary)—Activity programs. I. Title.
  PS3606.R433A73   2008
  812'.6—dc22   2008026295

British Library Cataloguing in Publication Data is available.

Library of Congress Catalog Card Number: 2008026295
ISBN: 978-1-59158-734-7

First published in 2008

Libraries Unlimited/Teacher Ideas Press, 88 Post Road West, Westport, CT 06881
A Member of the Greenwood Publishing Group, Inc.
www.teacherideaspress.com
www.lu.com

Printed in the United States of America

The paper used in this book complies with the
Permanent Paper Standard issued by the National
Information Standards Organization (Z39.48–1984).

10 9 8 7 6 5 4 3 2 1

Contents

Introduction

Say the words "Once upon a time . . ." to any adult, and you will probably see a smile slip across his or her face. Those are magical words—words that conjure up legends, fairy tales, and stories of long ago. For most of us, they bring back pleasant memories of someone (our parents or a favorite teacher) reading (aloud) a story or book. Those words may remind us of simpler times—times long before we had to worry about home mortgages, saving for our kids' college tuition, retirement plans, or even behavioral objectives. The memories were sweet and the recollections were always pleasurable.

Think how those same four words might affect the students with whom you work. Think of the mental journeys or creative adventures you can share with youngsters as you lead them through the magical world of children's literature. Imaginations are stimulated and minds are filled with the delicious sounds of language in action! It is that language—the language of feeling, emotion, and passion—that excites youngsters and helps them appreciate the role literature plays in their everyday lives (as it has for generations).

And what better way to bring children's literature alive than through the magic of readers theatre? Readers theatre offers youngsters interesting and unique insights into the utility of language and its value in both its printed and oral forms. It is "language arts" in its purest form: it boosts listening and speaking skills, enhances writing abilities, powers reading development, develops positive self-concepts, and transforms reluctant readers into energized readers. Quite simply, it is literature brought to life and life brought to literature.

STORYTELLING AND READERS THEATRE

The magic of storytelling has been a tradition of every culture and civilization since the dawn of language. It binds human beings and celebrates their heritage as no other language art can. It is part and parcel of the human experience, because it underscores the values and experiences we cherish as well as those we seek to share with each other. No where is this more important than in today's classroom or library. Perhaps it is a natural part of who we are that stories command our attention and help us appreciate the values, ideas, and traditions we hold dear. So too, should students have those same experiences and pleasures.

Storytelling conjures up all sorts of visions and possibilities: faraway lands, magnificent adventures, enchanted princes, beautiful princesses, evil wizards and wicked witches, a few dragons and demons, a couple of castles and cottages, perhaps a mysterious forest or two, and certainly tales of mystery, intrigue, and adventure. These are stories of tradition and timelessness, tales that enchant, mystify, and excite through a marvelous weaving of characters, settings, and plots that have stood the test of time. Our senses are stimulated, our mental images are energized, and our experiences are fortified through the magic of storytelling.

Storytelling is also a way of sharing the power and intrigue of language. I suppose part of my belief that storytelling is the quintessential classroom activity lies in the fact that it is an opportunity to bring life, vitality, and substance to the two-dimensional letters and words on a printed page. It is also an interpersonal activity, a "never-fail" way to connect with minds and souls and hearts.

When children are provided with regular opportunities to become storytellers, they develop a personal stake in the literature shared. They also begin to cultivate personal interpretations of that literature, which leads to higher levels of appreciation and comprehension. Practicing and performing stories is an involvement endeavor, one that demonstrates and utilizes numerous languaging activities.

Readers theatre is a storytelling device that stimulates the imagination and promotes *all* of the language arts. Simply stated, it is an oral interpretation of a piece of literature read in a dramatic style. Teachers all across the country have long promoted the powerful benefits of drama for their students: positive emotional growth, increased levels of motivation, and absolute engagement in the tasks of learning.

Readers theatre is an act of involvement, an opportunity to share, a time to creatively interact with others, and a personal interpretation of what can or could be. It provides numerous opportunities for youngsters to make stories and literature come alive and pulsate with their own unique brand of perception and vision. In so doing, literature becomes personal and reflective; children have a breadth of opportunities to be authentic users of language.

WHAT YOUR PRINCIPAL NEEDS TO KNOW

In this era of accountability and standards-based education, many educators want to know if classroom practices—whether traditional or innovative—have an impact on the literacy growth of students. Significant research on the use of readers theatre in elementary classrooms has demonstrated its positive effects on comprehension development, motivation to read, attitudes toward learning, and appreciation of reading as a lifelong skill.

What follows is a brief summary of some significant research on the impact of readers theatre on the literacy growth of students. Feel free to share this information with interested (or questioning) administrators, parents, or community members. Suffice it to say, readers theatre is a "research-based practice" that has been demonstrated to have a significant and powerful impact on students' reading growth and development.

❖ "Creative and critical thinking are enhanced through the utilization of readers theatre. Children are active participants in the interpretation and delivery of a story; as such, they develop thinking skills that are divergent rather than convergent, and interpretive skills that are supported rather than directed" (Fredericks 2007).

❖ "Readers theatre provides an active, analytical framework for reading and helps students to understand and interpret what they read" (Wolf 1998).

❖ "Readers theatre provides troubled readers with successful reading experiences; it can reshape images of failure into those of success and accomplishment. Readers theatre forms a bridge between troubled reading to supported reading, and ultimately, independent reading" (Dixon et al. 1996).

❖ "Readers theatre [promotes] oral reading fluency, as children [explore] and [interpret] the meaning of literature" (Martinez et al. 1999).

❖ "[W]e are gaining evidence from classroom research that readers theatre yields improvements in students' word recognition, fluency, and comprehension" (Rasinski 2003).

❖ "[Readers theatre] is valuable for non-English speaking children or non-fluent readers. Readers theatre provides them with positive models of language usage and interpretation. . . . It allows them to see 'language in action' and the various ways in which language can be used" (Fredericks 2001).

❖ "Even resistant readers eagerly engage in practicing for readers theatre performance, reading and rereading scripts many times" (Tyler & Chard 2000).

❖ "[Students] who did readers theatre on a regular basis made, on average, more than a year's growth in reading" (Strecker et al. 1999).

❖ "As students take on the roles of characters [in readers theatre], they also take on the roles of competent readers" (Fredericks 2008a, 2008b).

The research is clear: Classroom teachers and librarians who make readers theatre a regular and systematic component of their literacy instruction and introduction to literature will be providing those students with positive opportunities to succeed in all aspects of reading growth and development. Word recognition, vocabulary, fluency, and comprehension can all be enhanced considerably when readers theatre becomes part of the educational offerings in any classroom or library.

WHAT IS THE VALUE OF READERS THEATRE?

Above and beyond the substantive research supporting the use of readers theatre as a positive classroom and library activity, here's what I like so much about readers theatre: It allows children to breathe life and substance into literature, an interpretation that is neither right nor wrong, since it will be colored by kids' unique perspectives, experiences, and vision. The reader's interpretation of a piece of literature is intrinsically more valuable than some predetermined "translation" that might be found in a teacher's manual, for example.

Many teachers subscribe to the notion that reading involves an active and energetic relationship between the reader and the text. That is, the reader–text relationship is reciprocal and involves the characteristics of the reader as well as the nature of the materials (Fredericks 2001). This philosophy of reading has particular applications for teachers and librarians building effective literacy programs. It also serves as a foundation for the implementation and effectiveness of readers theatre.

With that in mind, here are some of the many educational values I see in readers theatre. These have come from my own work with youngsters as a former classroom teacher and reading specialist, a thorough review of the literature on readers theatre, as well as my observations of, and conversations with, classroom teachers throughout the United States and Canada.

1. Readers theatre brings literature to life! For many students, particularly those struggling with reading, words on a page often appear as "lifeless characters"—devoid of expression, emotion, or involvement. Readers theatre, however, provides both accomplished and struggling readers with a lively and active interpretation of books. Readers get to see and participate in a personal interpretation and involvement process that "activates" the words, characters, and plots of stories.

2. Students are connected to real literature in authentic situations. They are exposed to quality literature from a wide range of authors and a wide range of genres. Many readers theatre scripts are based on real literature sources, and students can begin developing their own interpretations of literature through the creation of their own scripts based on those books. In fact, one of the best ways to help children enjoy and extend their appreciation of good books is by encouraging them to write and perform readers theatre productions after reading an appropriate piece of literature. Readers theatre can also be used to introduce children to good literature. After performing a readers theatre script, children will be stimulated to read the original source, not to compare, but rather to extend their learning opportunities. Readers theatre may precede the reading of a related book or be used as an appropriate follow-up to the reading (oral or silent) of a good book. Quality literature and readers theatre are mutually complimentary elements of the overall literacy program that underscore children's active engagement in text.

3. Children can learn about the major features of children's literature: plot, theme, setting, point of view, and characterization. This occurs when they are provided with opportunities to design and construct their own readers theatre scripts (after experiencing prepared scripts such as those in this book or scripts that you create using books and literature shared in regular reading instruction).

4. Readers theatre helps students focus on the integration of all the language arts: reading, writing, speaking, and listening. Children begin to see that effective communication and the comprehension of text are inexorably intertwined. Most state standards in the language arts, and all research reports about best practices in literacy, underscore literacy as an integrated series of related components. In other words, literacy growth is not just growth in reading—it is the development of reading in concert with the other language arts. The section "Hey, What About Standards?" provides the specific connections between each of the English/Language Arts Standards and readers theatre. It's interesting to note how readers theatre promotes, enhances, and solidifies students' mastery of 11 of the 12 English/Language Arts Standards.

5. Teachers and librarians have also discovered that readers theatre is an excellent way to enhance the development of important communication skills. Voice projection, intonation, inflection, and pronunciation skills are all promoted throughout any readers theatre production. This places more of a value on the processes of literacy instruction than it does on the products (e.g., standardized test scores).

6. Readers theatre allows children to experience stories in a supportive and nonthreatening format that underscores their active involvement. This is particularly beneficial for those students who are struggling with reading. Struggling readers often envision reading as something "done *to* a text" rather than as something "done *with* a text." This shift in perspective is often a critical factor in the success youngsters can eventually enjoy in reading. A change in attitude, a change in viewpoints, and a change in purpose often lead below-level readers to some new and interesting discoveries. Motivation, confidence, and outlook are all positively affected when students become the players and the performers. Equally important, the development and enhancement of self-concept is facilitated through readers theatre. Because children are working in concert with other children in a supportive atmosphere, their self-esteem mushrooms accordingly.

7. Readers theatre stimulates the imagination and the creation of visual images. A process of mental imagery helps readers construct "mind pictures" that serve as a way to tie together predictions, background knowledge, and textual knowledge in a satisfying experience. Once images are created, they become a permanent part of long-term memory. Just as important, they assist in the development of independent readers who are "connected" with the stories they read. It has been substantiated that when youngsters are provided with opportunities to create their own mental images, their comprehension and appreciation of a piece of writing will be enhanced considerably.

8. The central goal of reading instruction is comprehension. Comprehension is based on one's ability to make sense of printed materials. It goes beyond one's ability to remember details or recall factual information from text. Several researchers (Wiggens & McTighe 1998; Wiske 1998) suggest that students comprehend when they are able to a) connect new knowledge to their prior knowledge, b) interpret what they learn, c) apply their knowledge to new situations, and d) explain and predict events and actions. Readers theatre provides students with rich opportunities to accomplish all four elements of reading comprehension in a learning environment that is both supportive and engaged. Giving meaning to print is one of the major results of readers theatre just as it is one of the major results of comprehension instruction.

9. Cunningham and Allington (2003) have shown that readers theatre is a perfect multilevel activity that allows teachers to group students heterogeneously rather than by ability, as is done in traditional reading programs. It provides teachers with varied options to group students by interest and desire rather than by reading level. Parts can be assigned that are sufficiently challenging (instructional level) without forcing students to deal with material at their frustration level of reading. Because students will have multiple opportunities to practice their "reading materials" at an appropriate level, they will be able to achieve both a level of competence and fluency not normally provided in more traditional "round robin" reading activities.

10. Readers theatre is a participatory event. The characters as well as the audience are all intimately involved in the design, structure, and delivery of the story. Children begin to realize that reading is not a solitary activity, but rather one that can be shared and discussed with others. As a result, readers theatre enhances the development of cooperative learning strategies. Not only does readers theatre require youngsters to work together toward a common goal, but even more important, it supports their efforts in doing so.

11. Because it is the performance that drives readers theatre, children are given more opportunities to invest themselves and their personalities in the production of a readers theatre. The same story may be subject to several different presentations depending on the group or the individual youngsters involved.

12. When children are provided with opportunities to write or script their own readers theatre, their writing abilities are supported and encouraged. As children become familiar with the design and format of readers theatre scripts, they can begin to utilize their creative talents in designing their own scripts. Readers theatre also exposes students to many examples of quality literature. That literature serves as positive models for their own writing. Just as authors of children's books write for authentic purposes (e.g., to entertain, to inform, to convince), so too will students understand the value of purposeful writing as they craft original readers theatre scripts or adaptations from popular books and stories.

13. Readers theatre is fun! Children of all ages have delighted in using readers theatre for many years. It is delightful and stimulating, encouraging and fascinating, relevant and personal. It is a classroom or library activity filled with a cornucopia of instructional possibilities and educational ventures.

"HEY, WHAT ABOUT STANDARDS?"

In response to a demand for a cohesive set of standards that address overall curriculum design and comprehensive student performance expectations in reading and language arts education, the International Reading Association, in concert with the National Council of Teachers of English, developed and promulgated the IRA/NCTE *Standards for the English Language Arts*. These standards provide a focused outline of the essential components of a well-structured language arts curriculum.

The 12 standards place an emphasis on literacy development as a lifelong process—one that starts well before youngsters enter school and continues throughout their lives. Thus, these standards are intentionally integrative and multidisciplinary. Just as important, they support and underscore the values of readers theatre (see above) as a multipurpose language arts activity—one appropriate for both classroom and library.

The chart on page xii provides an abridged version of the *Standards for the English Language Arts*. Along with each standard (as appropriate) is how readers theatre serves as a valuable and innovative teaching tool in support of those standards.

English/Language Arts Standards*	Readers Theatre Support
1. Students are engaged in a wide variety of print and nonprint resources.	Readers theatre introduces students to a wealth of literature from a variety of literary sources.
2. Students are exposed to many genres of literature.	Readers theatre offers students a range of reading materials that span the eight basic genres of children's literature.
3. Students use many reading strategies to comprehend text.	Readers theatre invites students to assume an active role in comprehension development through their engagement and participation.
4. Students communicate in a variety of ways.	Readers theatre invites students to practice reading, writing, listening, and speaking in an enjoyable and educative process.
5. Students learn through writing.	Readers theatre encourages students to develop their own scripts and share them with a receptive audience.
6. Students use a variety of language conventions to understand text.	Readers theatre encourages students to discuss and understand how language conveys ideas.
7. Students are involved in personally meaningful research projects.	Readers theatre invites youngsters to examine and explore stories from a wide range of perspectives.
8. Students are comfortable with technology.	
9. Students gain an appreciation of language in a variety of venues.	Readers theatre encourages students to look at language and language use in a host of educational formats.
10. Non-English-speaking students develop competencies in all the language arts.	Readers theatre offers models of English use in a fun and engaging format.
11. Students are members of a host of literacy communities.	Readers theatre provides creative, investigative, and dynamic opportunities to see language in action.
12. Students use language for personal reasons.	Readers theatre offers innumerable opportunities for students to engage in personally enriching language activities.

*Modified and abridged from *Standards for the English Language Arts*, International Reading Association/National Council of Teachers of English, 1996

When reviewing these standards, it should become evident that many elements can be promoted through the regular and systematic introduction of readers theatre into the elementary language arts curriculum. Equally important is that those standards assist teachers and librarians in validating the impact and significance of readers theatre as a viable and valuable instructional tool—in language arts and throughout the entire elementary curriculum.

PART I

READERS THEATRE IN THE CLASSROOM AND LIBRARY

CHAPTER 1

Getting Started with Readers Theatre

INTRODUCING READERS THEATRE TO STUDENTS

Ever since I wrote my first book of readers theatre scripts—*Frantic Frogs and Other Frankly Fractured Folktales for Readers Theatre* (1993)—I have been amazed by and delighted with the incredible response readers theatre has generated among educators across the country. Teachers in urban, suburban, and rural schools have all told me of the incredible power of readers theatre as a regular feature of their language arts or reading curricula. In more than one dozen subsequent books on readers theatre (please see "More Teacher Resources by Anthony D. Fredericks" at the end of this book) I have shared (and seen) the passion and excitement that are so much a part of a curriculum infused with readers theatre.

In the teacher in-service programs I conduct and conference workshops I lead, I continue to receive rave reviews of readers theatre as a way of helping students take an active role in the reading process. Many teachers have commented on the improved levels of motivation and heightened participation in all aspects of the reading curriculum when readers theatre has been added to students' daily literacy activities.

3

However, readers theatre is not something you just "drop into" the curriculum one day and expect students to enthusiastically embrace it. It must be introduced to students on a gradual basis —over the course of several days or several weeks—to achieve maximum impact. Of course no two teachers will introduce readers theatre in exactly the same way. What follows is an instructional plan of action that allows for a great deal of latitude and variation depending on how your reading or language arts program is organized as well as the specific time constraints of your classroom schedule. Feel free to make any necessary adjustments or modifications in the schedule to suit your personal philosophy or the specific instructional needs of your students.

My experience, as well as that of many teachers, is that students need to transition through four stages in order for readers theatre to become a viable component of the overall literacy program. These four stages follow:

- **Introduction.** This is the stage at which students are first introduced to readers theatre. In cases where most of the students in your class have been using readers theatre in previous grades, this stage can be eliminated.

- **Familiarization.** In this stage students become comfortable with the concept of readers theatre. They begin to understand its value as an instructional tool as well as its worth in helping them become accomplished and fluent readers.

- **Practice.** Here students are offered a variety of ways in which to practice readers theatre in authentic situations. Students begin to see positive growth and development in both reading fluency and comprehension.

- **Integration.** This stage provides students with regular and systematic opportunities to use readers theatre as a significant element in other aspects of the reading program (e.g., guided reading, literature circles) as well as other subject areas (e.g., science, social studies).

What follows are some suggested instructional activities and presentations to share with your students. These suggestions are general in nature and can be easily incorporated into one or more lesson plans. Again, depending on the dynamics of your overall classroom reading program or library program, the lessons may last for as little as 10 minutes or as much as one hour.

1. **Introduction** (suggested duration: 1–3 days)

   A.   Select a prepared readers theatre script. Choose one of the scripts from this book or from any other readers theatre collection of scripts. Duplicate sufficient copies of the script for every member of the class.

   B.   Distribute the scripts to students. Tell students that a readers theatre script is exactly like a script used by actors and actors in television, the movies, or plays. The only difference is that in readers theatre the lines don't have to be memorized. Nevertheless, they still have to be read with the same level of enthusiasm and emotion that professional actors use.

   C.   Identify and discuss the various printed elements of the script. Identify the narrator, the staging instructions, how the various actor parts are designated, any emotional suggestions noted for specific characters, and other features.

   D.   Invite students to silently read through the script on their own. You may wish to use the script as part of a guided reading lesson. Afterward, ask student to share what they noted in the script (e.g., a narrator, a different style of writing, short parts and long parts). Record students' observations on the chalkboard and plan time to discuss each of their suggestions.

E. Use the script as a read-aloud for your students. Tell students that you are going to model how a readers theatre script should be read. Inform them that you will also be modeling fluent and expressive reading. You will add emotion to certain parts and will maintain a consistent rate throughout the reading, as well. Invite students to listen carefully to this initial reading.

F. After reading through the script, invite students to discuss what they heard. How did your reading differ from other read-alouds in the classroom? How was it similar? What did they enjoy about your reading? How might they have presented the script? Record their observations on the chalkboard.

G. As appropriate, show students another prepared readers theatre script. Invite them to identify selected elements of the script (narrator, specific characters, staging directions, etc.). Make sure students understand that most readers theatre scripts follow a fairly standard format.

2. **Familiarization** (suggested duration: 1 week)

Before engaging students in this stage you may wish to select 8 to 10 lines or passages from the forthcoming script. It is suggested that these lines or passages come from the beginning of the script and that they be representative of most (if not all) of the characters (including any narrator(s)). Record these passages on cardboard sentence strips (using block printing or a word processing program).

Here are some sample sentence strips from the beginning of the readers theatre script "John Henry" (see part II):

CHORUS	Oh, my hammer, Hammer ring, While I sing, Lawd, Hear me sing!

NARRATOR 1	There's this story—a true story I hear tell—been around the hills of West Virginia for many years. It's the story of John Henry—John Henry, the best steel driving man in the whole country.

NARRATOR 2	Yup, that steel drivin' man was the best there ever was. He could hammer for hours without missing a beat. He could hammer better and faster than any four men put together. His hammer was so fast he had to cool it down with a bucket of water every 15 minutes just so a fire wouldn't start.

NARRATOR 1	All the railroad bosses wanted John Henry to work for them 'cause he was the best there ever was. Yes, he was the best there ever was.

CHORUS	Ain't no hammer.
	Rings like mine,
	Rings like gold, Lawd,
	Ain't it fine?
	Rings like silver,
	Peal on peal,
	Into the rock, Lawd,
	Drive the steel.
	If'n I dies, Lawd,
	I command
	Bury the hammer
	In my hand

After creating the necessary sentence strips engage students in the following sequence of activities:

A. Select a prepared readers theatre script (one from this book or any other collection of scripts). Record the script on audiotape (you may wish to alter your voice slightly for each of the characters or enlist the aid of some other teachers, or parents, to help you record the script). Make sure this recording of the script is fluent and smooth (practice several times if necessary).

B. Provide students with copies of the selected script. Point out, once more, how a readers theatre script is organized (e.g., narrator, individual characters, etc.). Tell them that they will listen to a reading of the script on an audiotape.

C. Play the recording for students. Invite them to listen carefully for the smooth and fluent reading. Encourage them, as appropriate, to follow along by pointing to each of the words as they hear it.

D. You may wish to repeat the sequence above, particularly if you are using this sequence with a group of struggling readers who may need some additional reinforcement and assistance.

E. Provide an opportunity for students to discuss what they heard, the intonation exhibited by the readers, the smoothness of their delivery, or any other aspects of the recording. You may wish to record these observations on the chalkboard or a sheet of newsprint.

F. Invite the class (or group) to read through the entire script chorally. You should also participate in this choral reading so that students have a positive model and an appropriate support system for their oral reading. At this stage, it would be appropriate to emphasize the emotions that selected characters may bring to their parts (e.g., anger, disgust, happiness).

G. After the choral reading, randomly distribute the sentence strips to selected students. Inform the students that they will now become the characters in the play. Invite the students to stand in a line. Point to each character (using the sequence in the script) and invite each student to read his or her selected passage.

H.   Invite other students to listen and comment (in a positive way) about the presentation of the first part of the script.

I.   Distribute the sentence strips to another group of students and invite them to line up and recite the passages as the previous group did. Again, it would be appropriate to discuss the nature of the presentation in a supportive atmosphere.

J.   (optional) Play the recorded version of the script again for the students. Invite them to make any additional comments.

3.   **Practice** (suggested duration: 1–2 weeks)

A.   Select, duplicate, and distribute a prepared script to all the students in your class. *Note:* At this particular stage I have frequently given students a selection of possible scripts from which the entire class makes a single choice. This gives students a sense of ownership over the script, which ultimately results in a heightened level of motivation.

B.   Divide the class into pairs or triads of students. Invite students to share the script in their small groups. Students may wish to read the script silently, after which they may discuss the story line, characters, plot, or other elements. Students may also elect to read certain sections to each other, not only to practice fluent reading, but also to get a "feel" for the story.

C.   Assign roles. I like to assign one student from each of the small groups to a character in the script. (If there are, for example, six characters, I make sure that students are initially divided into six small groups). Each character then practices his or her part with the other members of his or her group (for example, the character reads only his or her own lines to group members, who assist with any difficult words or comment on the fluency of the reading).

D.   When students have had sufficient practice, arrange them according to the staging directions for that script.

E.   Invite the assigned students to read through the script just as they practiced it. Invite others students to listen to the presentation. After the script is completed, discuss how it might be improved the next time.

F.   (optional) Reassign roles to different students in the class. Divide the class into small groups and repeat the sequence as described above.

4.   **Integration** (suggested duration: remainder of the school year or remainder of the unit)

A.   Select a prepared readers theatre script (one from this book or any other collection of scripts). Assign roles to selected students and distribute copies of the scripts to those students. You may wish to use two or three separate scripts—each distributed to a different group of students in the class.

B.   Invite students to practice their assigned parts in preparation for a production later on. Students should be provided with practice time in class and should also be encouraged to practice their respective parts at home.

C.   Schedule a day and time when students will present their scripts to others in the class. This initial presentation should be kept as an in-class one to allay any fears students may have about presenting to an unfamiliar group of individuals. Ask students if they would like to invite their parents to attend this presentation.

D.   After presenting the initial script, invite students to select other prepared scripts for a more formal presentation.

E.   Invite students to create their own readers theatre scripts from self-selected literature in the classroom or school library. Make this process a normal part of your writing program or a basic element of a writer's workshop. After students have created their own scripts, provide them with opportunities to present them to appropriate audiences, including classrooms at a grade level above or below yours.

F.   Consider the implementation of readers theatre as a fundamental element in literature circles. After students have engaged in a discussion about a self-selected book, invite them to develop the book into a readers theatre script that may become a permanent part of the classroom library.

G.   Students may wish to use readers theatre as part of a thematic unit. According to Meinbach et al., "a thematic approach to learning combines structured, sequential, and well-organized strategies, activities, children's literature, and materials used to expand a particular concept" (2000, 10). Readers theatre has the advantage of offering youngsters a creative and dynamic way to utilize their reading abilities in a productive and engaging way. By integrating readers theatre into thematic units, you will help students gain a deeper appreciation of the role of reading (and reading fluency) in their overall literacy development.

H.   Use prepared scripts or student-created scripts as part of your content area instruction. Readers theatre has been shown to stimulate curiosity (when used in advance of a content area unit) and promote enthusiasm (when used as part of an instructional unit), particularly when incorporated into a variety of subject areas (Fredericks 2007).

I.   Readers theatre can be effectively incorporated into guided reading activities in any classroom. The three critical and interrelated stages of guided reading (before reading, during reading, and after reading) offer you and your students unique opportunities to weave readers theatre into the overall reading curriculum. Imagine the thrill and excitement of students using a self-designed script as the reading selection in a guided reading group! Readers theatre holds the promise of helping students in a guided reading group understand and appreciate the richness of language, the ways in which to interpret that language, and how language can be a powerful vehicle for the comprehension and appreciation of different forms of literature (Fredericks 2001).

CHAPTER 2

Performing Readers Theatre for an Audience

One of the features of readers theatre I enjoy very much is the many ways in which it can become part of the classroom curriculum. Along with scores of other teachers, I've discovered that readers theatre can be a wonderful way for students to become active participants in the entire learning process as well as a delightful exploration of every curricular area.

Obviously readers theatre achieves its greatest potency when students have multiple opportunities to share it with others. This chapter focuses on ways you can make that experience incredibly successful.

SCRIPT PREPARATION

One of the advantages of using readers theatre in the classroom or library is the lack of extra work or preparation time necessary to get "up and running." If you use the scripts in this book, your preparation time will be minimal.

❖ After a script has been selected for presentation, make sufficient copies. A copy of the script should be provided for each actor. In addition, making two or three extra copies (one for you and "replacement" copies for scripts that are accidentally damaged or lost) is also a good idea. Copies for the audience are unnecessary and are not suggested.

9

❖ Bind each script between two sheets of colored construction paper or poster board. Bound scripts tend to formalize the presentation a little and lend an air of professionalism to the actors.

❖ Highlight each character's speaking parts with different color highlighter pens. This helps youngsters track their parts without being distracted by the dialogue of others.

STARTING OUT

Introducing the concept of readers theatre to students for the first time may be as simple as sharing a script with an entire class and "walking" youngsters through the design and delivery of that script.

❖ Emphasize that a readers theatre performance does not require any memorization of the script. The interpretation and performance are whatcount.

❖ Read an entire script aloud, taking on the various roles. Let students know how easy and comfortable this process is.

❖ Encourage selected volunteers to read assigned parts of a sample script to the entire class. Readers should stand or sit in a circle so that other classmates can observe them.

❖ Provide opportunities for additional re-readings using other volunteers. Plan time to discuss the ease of presentation and the different interpretations offered by various readers.

❖ Allow readers an opportunity to practice their script before presenting it to an audience. Take some time to discuss voice intonation, facial gestures, body movements, and other features that could be used to enhance the presentation.

❖ Give children the opportunity to suggest their own modifications, adaptations, or interpretations of the script. They will undoubtedly be "in tune" with the interests and perceptions of their peers and can offer some distinctive and personal interpretations.

❖ Encourage students to select nonstereotypical roles within any readers theatre script. For example, boys may take on female roles and girls may take on male roles, the smallest person in the class may take on the role of a giant fire-breathing dragon (for example), or a shy student may take on the role of a boastful, bragging giant. Provide sufficient opportunities for students to expand and extend their appreciation of readers theatre through a variety of "out of character" roles.

STAGING

Staging involves the physical location of the readers as well as any necessary movements. Unlike a more formal play, the movements are often minimal. The emphasis is more on presentation, less on action.

❖ For most presentations, readers will stand or sit on stools or chairs. The physical location of each reader has been indicated for each of the scripts in this book.

❖ If there are many characters in the presentation, it may be advantageous to have characters in the rear (upstage) standing while those in the front (downstage) are seated on stools or chairs. This ensures that the audience will both see and hear every actor.

❖ Usually all of the characters will be on stage throughout the duration of the presentation. For most it is not necessary to have characters enter and exit. If you seat the characters on stools, they may face the audience when they are involved in a particular scene and then turn around whenever they are not involved in a scene.

❖ Make simple hand-lettered signs with the name of each character. Loop a piece of string or yarn through each sign and hang it around the neck of each respective character. That way, the audience will know the identity of each character throughout the presentation.

❖ Each reader will have her or his own copy of the script in a paper cover (see above). If possible, use a music stand for each reader's script (this allows readers to use their hands for dramatic interpretations as necessary).

❖ Several presentations have a narrator to set up the story. The narrator serves to establish the place and time of the story for the audience so that the characters can "jump into" their parts from the beginning. Typically, the narrator is separated from the other "actors" and can be identified by a simple sign.

PROPS

Two positive features of readers theatre are its ease of preparation and its ease of presentation. Informality is a hallmark of any readers theatre script.

❖ Much of the setting for a story should take place in the audience's mind. Elaborate scenery is not necessary; simple props are often the best. For example:

– A branch or potted plant may serve as a tree.

– A drawing on the chalkboard may illustrate a building.

– A hand-lettered sign may designate one part of the staging area as a particular scene (e.g., swamp, castle, field, forest).

– Children's toys may be used for uncomplicated props (e.g., telephone, vehicles, etc.).

– A sheet of aluminum foil or a remnant of blue cloth may be used to simulate a lake or pond.

❖ Costumes for the actors are unnecessary. A few simple items may be suggested by students. For example:

– Hats, scarves, or aprons may be used by major characters.

– A paper cutout may serve as a tie, button, or badge.

– Old clothing (borrowed from parents) may be used as warranted.

❖ Some teachers and librarians have discovered that the addition of appropriate background music or sound effects enhances a readers theatre presentation.

❖ It's important to remember that the emphasis in readers theatre is on the reading, not on any accompanying "features." The best presentations are often the simplest.

DELIVERY

I've often found it useful to let students know that the only difference between a readers theatre presentation and a movie role is that they will have a script in their hands. This allows them to focus more on presenting a script rather than on memorizing it.

❖ When first introduced to readers theatre, students often have a tendency to "read into" their scripts. Encourage students to look up from their scripts and interact with other characters or the audience as appropriate.

❖ Practicing the script beforehand can eliminate the problem of students burying their heads in the pages. Children will understand the need to involve the audience as much as possible in the development of the story.

❖ Voice projection and delivery are important in allowing the audience to understand character actions. The proper mood and intent need to be established, which is possible when children are familiar and comfortable with each character's "style."

❖ Again, the emphasis is on delivery, so be sure to suggest different types of voice (i.e., angry, irritated, calm, frustrated, excited, etc.) that children may wish to use for their particular character(s).

SCRIPT SELECTION

One of the best presentation options is when several groups of students in your classroom come together to present a selection of readers theatre scripts for an audience of enthusiastic students (from the same or a different grade) and some very appreciative parents. Here are some points for you to consider:

❖ When possible, invite students to select a variety of scripts to be included in the presentation. Inform them that a combination of short scripts and longer scripts adds variety to the program. When students are invited to be part of the selection process a sense of "ownership" develops, which contributes to the ultimate success of the overall presentation(s).

❖ Consider the age and grade of the audience. For younger students (grades K–2) the total program should be no longer than 25 minutes (a mix of three to five scripts). For older students (grades 3–6) the total program should be no longer than 45 minutes (a mix of five to seven scripts).

❖ If feasible, include a section of the program (parts of a script or an entire production) in which the audience takes an active role. This could include singing, clapping, repeating selected lines in a production (provide cue cards), or some other physical contribution. This would be particularly appropriate for younger audiences, whose attention span is typically short and sporadic.

"IT'S SHOW TIME!"

After scripts have been selected by you and your students, it's time to consider how, when, and where you would like to present them. There are many options to consider. The following list, which is not all-inclusive, includes a variety of presentation options for readers theatre. How you and your students present readers theatre will ultimately be determined by the nature of your overall reading program, the time and facilities available, the comfort level of students, and the demands of your curriculum. You will discover that there is an almost inexhaustible array of options available.

Suggested Presentation Options for Readers Theatre

❖ One group of students presents a script to another group.

❖ One group of students presents to the entire class.

❖ Several groups of students present to the entire class (an in-class "readers theatre festival").

❖ One group of students presents to another class at the same grade level.

❖ Several groups of students present to another class at the same grade level.

❖ One group of students presents to a class at a higher or lower grade level.

❖ Several groups of students present to a class at a higher or lower grade level.

❖ One group of students presents to the entire school (at an all-school assembly).

❖ Several groups of students present to the entire school (at an all-school assembly).

❖ One group of students in the class presents to an audience of parents, school personnel, the school principal, and other interested individuals.

❖ Several groups of students in the class present to an audience of parents, school personnel, the school principal, and other interested individuals.

❖ One group of students produces a readers theatre script that is videotaped and distributed throughout the school and/or district.

❖ Several groups of students produce a readers theatre script that is videotaped and distributed throughout the school and/or district.

❖ Students join with students from another class to co-present readers theatre scripts at a grade level or an all-school literacy celebration.

It is important to share some of these options with your students and invite them to identify those with which they would be most comfortable. My rule of thumb is to "start small" at first—for example, have one or two groups of students present to the class as part of a regularly scheduled readers theatre presentation time (once a month, for example). As students gain confidence and self-assurance, they should be encouraged to take their presentations "on the road," sharing them with other classes and other grades.

INVITING AN AUDIENCE

An audience gives readers theatre legitimacy—it is a signal to students that all their hard work and practice has a purpose: to share the fruits of their labors (and their concomitant improvements in reading fluency) with an appreciative group of individuals.

❖ Consider sending announcements or invitations to parents and other interested individuals. You may wish to design these yourself or, better yet, invite students to design, illustrate, and produce the invitations.

❖ In addition to parents, I have always found it appropriate (and exciting) to invite other adults with whom the students are familiar, including the school secretary, the custodian, a bus driver or two, cafeteria workers, and aides, for example. After the presentation the students are sure to get a raft of positive comments and lots of appreciation from these individuals as they encounter them throughout the school.

❖ As appropriate, invite community members to be part of the audience. Residents of a local senior citizen center or retirement home are a most logical (and very enthusiastic) audience. These folks are always appreciative of the work of children and are often eager to see what is happening in the local schools.

POST-PRESENTATION

As a wise author once said, "The play's the thing." So it is with readers theatre. In other words, the mere act of presenting a readers theatre script is complete in and of itself. It is not necessary, or even required, to do any type of formalized evaluation after readers theatre. Once again, the emphasis is on informality. Readers theatre should and can be a pleasurable and stimulating experience for children.

Following are a few ideas you may want to share with students. In doing so, you will be providing youngsters with important learning opportunities that extend and promote all aspects of your reading and language arts program.

❖ After a presentation, discuss with students how the script enhanced or altered the original story.

❖ Invite students to suggest other characters who could be added to the script.

❖ Invite students to suggest alternate dialogue for various characters.

❖ Invite students to suggest different setting(s) for the script.

❖ Invite students to talk about their reactions to various characters' expressions, tone of voice, presentations, or dialogues.

❖ After a presentation, invite youngsters to suggest modifications they think could be made to the script.

PART II

FOLKLORE, LEGENDS, AND TALL TALES

CHAPTER 3

Heroes and Heroines

America is a country of heroes and heroines. We love our heroes and we love what they do—whether the tales of what they do are entirely truthful or just slightly believable. Heroes give us strength and something to strive for. They are icons and they are real, simply because they embody what we wish to celebrate: strength, desire, honor, courage, determination, and a dozen other attributes that we cherish. Perhaps our heroes have one or two flaws, but that's OK, because with a little massaging and embellishment we can make our heroes and heroines seem just a little larger than they really were.

American folklore is filled with heroes of every conceivable shape and size. They come from every generation and are a part of every aspect of our country's history. They are as much a part of our culture as "mom, baseball, and apple pie." No matter what the challenge or the danger, there is always a hero or heroine who will come to our rescue or who will save the day. We adore them, we welcome them, and we celebrate their impact on our everyday (and perhaps mundane) lives.

THE LEGEND OF CASEY JONES

Casey Jones and his fateful ride one dark rainy night has become a staple of American storytelling. There was an actual "Casey Jones," one John Luther Jones from Cayce, Kentucky (hence the nickname "Casey"). Mr. Jones was a railroad man and was involved in a terrible locomotive crash on the night of April 30, 1900. Several of the people on the train that night survived and told the story of Casey's courage and bravery. As many legends have been, this one was supplanted with additional

17

details and a few embellishments to create the tale we know today, which, although not entirely truthful, remains believable nonetheless.

JOHN HENRY

There is some disagreement about whether John Henry was a real person or not. Suffice it to say, he stood for all the railroad workers who, in the years after the Civil War, began to lay tracks across this country. Many of those miles of tracks had to be laid in tunnels cut through hard mountain shale, and that took a special kind of worker—one who was tough, determined, and hearty. John Henry was just that sort of man. Whether he was real or not, he has long been an enduring character in American folklore—one who personifies the strength of a new nation and the resilience of steel.

JOHNNY APPLESEED

John Chapman (aka Johnny Appleseed) was born in Massachusetts in the late 1700s. Early in his life he moved to the Ohio Valley and began to plant apple orchards. He traveled throughout the Midwest—principally in Ohio, Illinois, and Indiana—to sow apple seeds and meet with travelers throughout the region. When he died in 1845 he was praised before Congress for his "labor of love." Many years later fictional details were added to his life and many liberties were taken with his travels, until he has become the icon he is today—a slightly different individual than he was in real life.

SWEET BETSY FROM PIKE

This story was a popular song with the forty-niners—those intrepid travelers who journeyed across the vast American West to seek their fortune in the gold fields of California in the mid-1800s. The "Pike" in this story refers to Pike County, Missouri. Many Californians tagged settlers from the Midwest as "Pikes" whether they came from Missouri or somewhere else. The term was often derogatory, indicating an individual of limited means and intelligence. "Pikes" were the butt of many jokes and numerous anecdotes. This readers theatre version uses verses from the song interspersed with several narrative interpretations.

The Legend of Casey Jones

STAGING: All the characters should be placed behind lecterns or music stands. If possible, provide each of the two engineers with engineer's hats or scarves around their necks. *Note:* The audience has a small part at the end of this script.

```
Narrator 1          Narrator 2          Narrator 3          Narrator 4
   X                   X                   X                   X
        Engineer 1              Engineer 2
           X                       X
```

ENGINEER 1: Well, the way I hear it, the best train man ever to work the tracks was good old Casey Jones.

ENGINEER 2: You got that right. Casey Jones was the best engineer in the land. Why, men would beg to work his train for him. He was a good man to work for. As long as you kept the boiler fired up, he would be your friend. A good man he was.

ENGINEER 1: Yup, that Casey Jones was a good man, that's for sure.

ENGINEER 2: There was one thing, however, that good old Casey never tolerated. He could never stand a slow train.

ENGINEER 1: You got that right!

ENGINEER 2: Yes sir, old Casey just couldn't stand being late. Heck, he would do everything possible to keep his train on time. Nothin' he hated more than a slow train or a late train. Just bothered him something terrible to be on a train that wasn't keepin' its time. Casey just figured that one slow train would slow down all the other trains. And he wasn't about to have his train be the one to hold up everyone else's train.

ENGINEER 1: That's about right. Why, he'd have everyone work those boilers stockin' wood so fast just to make up a minute . . . just to make up 30 seconds . . . just to make up a mite of time so's he wouldn't be the one to hold up everyone else on the line. Yup, that Casey Jones sure knew the value of stayin' on time.

ENGINEER 2: But I reckon that his timeliness was what killed him, too.

ENGINEER 1: Yup. I think you're right. Seems like he never could cotton to a slow train . . . a delayed train . . . and I reckon that's what did him in on the night of April 30, 1900.

ENGINEER 2: Yup, I remember it well. It was a rainy night . . . a night full of rain. 'Course it had been rainin' for quite some time in these here parts. Better part of five or six weeks we'd seen nothin' but rain . . . nothin' but rain coming down and spreadin' out over the land like some kind of flood.

ENGINEER 1: You got that right. But say, you know what?

ENGINEER 2: What?

ENGINEER 1: We got these here folks [points to the four narrators] standin' behind us, and I'll bet you a plug nickel that they've got a story to tell about Casey Jones.

ENGINEER 2: I reckon you're right. So why don't we let them tell the tale?

ENGINEER 1: And what a tale it is! It's "The Ballad of Casey Jones," and it's the truest story you'll ever hear. [exit stage right]

ENGINEER 2: So listen up close and listen up good. 'Cause they're ain't no better man than Casey Jones, and there ain't no better tale than "The Ballad of Casey Jones." [exit stage left]

NARRATOR 1: [in a sing-song voice] Come all you rounders if you want to hear,
The story of a brave engineer.

NARRATOR 2: Casey Jones was the rounder's name,
A high right-wheeler of mighty fame.

NARRATOR 3: Caller called Casey about half-past four;
He kissed his wife at the station door,

NARRATOR 4: Climbed into the cab with his orders in his hand,
Says, "This is my trip to the Holy Land."

NARRATOR 1: Through South Memphis yards on the fly,
He heard the fireman say, "You've got a white eye."

NARRATOR 2: All the switchmen knew by the engine's moan,
That the man at the throttle was Casey Jones.

NARRATOR 3: It had been raining some five or six weeks;
The railroad track was like the bed of a creek.

NARRATOR 4: They rated him down to a 30-mile gait;
Threw the southbound mail some eight hours late.

NARRATOR 1: Fireman says, "Casey, you're running too fast,
You ran the block board the last station we passed."

NARRATOR 2: Casey says, "Yes, I believe we'll make it through,
For she steams better than I ever knew."

NARRATOR 3: Casey says, "Fireman, don't you fret.
Keep knocking at the fire door; don't give up yet.

NARRATOR 4: I'm going to run her till she leaves the rail
Or make it on time with the southern mail."

NARRATOR 1: Around the curve and down the dump,
Two locomotives were bound to bump.

NARRATOR 2: Fireman hollered, "Casey, it's just ahead!
We might jump and make it, but we'll all be dead!"

NARRATOR 3: 'Twas round this curve he spied a passenger train.
Rousing his engine, he caused the bell to ring.

NARRATOR 4: Fireman jumped off, but Casey stayed on.
He's a good engineer, but he's dead and gone.

NARRATOR 1: Poor Casey Jones was all right,
For he stuck to his duty both day and night.

NARRATOR 2: They loved to hear the whistle and ring of No. 3,
As he came into Memphis on the old IC.

NARRATOR 3: Headaches and heartaches and all kinds of pain,
Are not apart from a railroad train.

NARRATOR 4: Tales that are earnest, noble, and grand
Belong to the life of a railroad man.

ALL: Tales that are earnest, noble, and grand
Belong to the life of a railroad man.

AUDIENCE: Tales that are earnest, noble, and grand
Belong to the life of a railroad man.

John Henry

STAGING: The characters should all be at lecterns or podiums. John Henry should be in the center of the staging area. If possible, provide John Henry with a hammer to hold in one hand throughout the presentation. The chorus should be to the rear of the staging area.

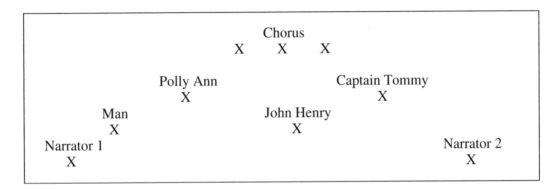

CHORUS: Oh, my hammer,
Hammer ring,
While I sing, Lawd,
Hear me sing!

NARRATOR 1: There's this story—a true story I hear tell—been around the hills of West Virginia for many years. It's the story of John Henry—John Henry, the best steel-driving man in the whole country.

NARRATOR 2: Yup, that steel-drivin' man was the best there ever was. He could hammer for hours without missing a beat. He could hammer better and faster than any four men put together. His hammer was so fast he had to cool it down with a bucket of water every 15 minutes just so a fire wouldn't start.

NARRATOR 1: All the railroad bosses wanted John Henry to work for them 'cause he was the best there ever was. Yes, he was the best there ever was.

CHORUS: Ain't no hammer
Rings like mine,
Rings like gold, Lawd,
Ain't it fine?

Rings like silver,
Peal on peal,
Into the rock, Lawd,
Drive the steel.

If'n I dies, Lawd,
I command:
Bury the hammer
In my hand.

NARRATOR 2: Well, one day the old Chesapeake and Ohio Railroad started making a tunnel in the Allegheny Mountains. The boss man—Captain Tommy—wanted the best there was. He wanted John Henry to work for him.

CAPTAIN TOMMY: John Henry, I hear that you're the best steel-drivin' man there is.

JOHN HENRY: You heard right. I'm the biggest, the strongest, and the best steel-drivin' man there ever was. What you heard is true.

CAPTAIN TOMMY: Then I want you to work for me. I want you to lead the men through the mountain. I want you to build me a tunnel through this mountain so that the train can come through here on its way to the great Wild West. John Henry, I want you to build me a tunnel.

JOHN HENRY: That I will, boss, that I will.

NARRATOR 1: So John Henry picked up not one, but two, steel hammers—one in each hand—and he commenced to swinging. He commenced to swinging so hard and so fast that the tunnel was five feet into the mountain before the lunch bell rang. But John Henry didn't stop for lunch. No, he continued to work. He continued to swing those hammers. He continued to build that tunnel. Yep, he was the best steel-driving man there ever was.

CHORUS: Oh, my hammer,
Hammer ring,
While I sing, Lawd,
Hear me sing!

NARRATOR 2: Now, that was a hot summer. It was a hot summer in West Virginia that year. Men dropped like flies in the summer heat. But not John Henry. John Henry jus' kept swinging those hammers through the heat of the day. While other men took a break, John Henry—his muscles rippling all across his body—jus' kept swinging those hammers. Yup, John Henry was a steel-drivin' man.

NARRATOR 1: Well, one day in the heat of the August sun a man appeared at the entrance to the tunnel. He had a machine with him, a special machine.

MAN: Hey, come on, everybody I got me a special machine. This here's a steam drill. It can drill holes faster than a dozen men working together. Yes sir, this here's the best thing that's ever happened in these here parts.

CAPTAIN TOMMY: I jus' don't know 'bout that. I got me the best steel-drivin' man in seven counties workin' right here. I got me John Henry working on this tunnel. Yup, John Henry, why, he could beat a dozen men workin' together. He's the best there ever was.

MAN: That sounds impossible. Nobody's that good! But I'll tell you what, if Mr. John Henry is faster than my steam driller, I'll give you this here machine for free.

CAPTAIN TOMMY: Hey, John Henry, this man says that his machine is better than you. He says his machine can work faster than you. He thinks his machine is better than you. What do you say to a contest?

25

NARRATOR 2: Now John Henry wasn't just the strongest man in seven counties, he was a pretty smart man, too. As he looked at that steam machine he saw the future. He saw a whole lot of steam machines drillin' tunnels all across the US of A. He saw a whole bunch of steam machines puttin' him and his friends out of work. He saw men out of jobs, out of work, and out of luck. He knew he had to do something to save his friends and their jobs.

JOHN HENRY: I'll take that challenge. I'd rather die with a hammer in my hand than let some steam drillin' machine beat me down.

CHORUS: Ain't no hammer
Rings like mine.
Rings like gold, Lawd,
Ain't it fine?

Rings like silver,
Peal on peal,
Into the rock, Lawd,
Drive the steel.

If'n I dies, Lawd,
I command:
Bury the hammer
In my hand.

NARRATOR 1: Soon as word got out 'bout the contest 'tween John Henry and the steam machine, people came from miles around to see it with their own eyes. Yup, it was another hot day in the West Virginia hills as John Henry and the steam machine stood side by side waitin' for the big race to start.

NARRATOR 2: Then "BANG," the race was on! At first the steam drill drove the steel twice as fast as John Henry. But John Henry picked up another hammer in his hand and commenced to working with two hammers. Blow after blow he struck away at the side of the mountain. Blow after blow he cut into the side of the mountain.

NARRATOR 1: Faster and faster John Henry drilled into the side of the mountain. Faster and faster John Henry moved in front of the steam drill. John Henry's hammer sounded like 10,000 hammers echoing throughout the tunnel. For six hours . . . seven hours . . . eight hours he hammered his way into the mountain. . . . He hammered his way in front of the steam drill.

NARRATOR 2: The crowd cheered. The crowd screamed. John Henry could not be stopped. Each of his hammers glowed white-hot as he tunneled deeper and deeper into the mountain. He was drivin' that steel faster and better than any machine.

CHORUS: Oh, my hammer,
Hammer ring.
While I sing, Lawd,
Hear me sing!

NARRATOR 1: Finally, at the ninth hour of the contest the steam drill jus' up and broke down. It was all over. The contest was over.

CAPTAIN TOMMY: I proclaim John Henry the winner of the contest. Ol' John Henry beat that steam machine. He beat that steam drill fair and square. He went farther into the mountain than the steam drill. He is the best! He is the best there ever was!

NARRATOR 2: The crowd cheered! The crowd yelled! But when they quieted down they heard another sound. They heard a scream. It was the scream of Polly Ann, John Henry's wife.

POLLY ANN: John Henry, John Henry. John Henry, don't go!

NARRATOR 1: John Henry lay on the ground. His heart had burst. His blood ran red over the dirt.

POLLY ANN: John Henry, John Henry. John Henry, don't go!

JOHN HENRY: A man ain't nothin' but a man. 'Fore I let that steam drill beat me, I'll die with a hammer in my hand. Yes, I will. I'll die with a hammer in my hand.

NARRATOR 2: That day, they carried John Henry down from the mountain. They carried him to the river and buried him with a hammer in each hand and a rod of steel across his chest. They put a pick and shovel at his head and they put a pick and shovel at his feet. That day, they buried the best steel-drivin' man there ever was. Yup, they buried the best steel-drivin' man there ever was!

CHORUS: Ain't no hammer
Rings like mine.
Rings like gold, Lawd,
Ain't it fine?

Rings like silver,
Peal on peal,
Into the rock, Lawd,
Drive the steel.

If'n I dies, Lawd,
I command:
Bury the hammer
In my hand.
Yes, bury the hammer
In my hand.

Johnny Appleseed

STAGING: The two narrators and each of the characters (with the exception of Johnny Appleseed) should be seated on tall stools or high chairs. They should each hold a copy of the script. Johnny Appleseed should also have a script and may walk around the staging area throughout the production.

```
        Amy              Nathaniel        Jim
         X                   X             X

                  John (Johnny Appleseed)
                           X
  Narrator 1                               Narrator 2
     X                                         X
```

NARRATOR 1: There's a story going around Ohio and Pennsylvania about a man called Johnny Appleseed. Seems he lived a long time ago—long about the early 1800s. Did some pretty amazing things, too.

NARRATOR 2: Yup, he sure did. We know that his given name was John Chapman and that he was born somewhere near Boston around 1775.

NARRATOR 1: He had himself a brother—man by the name of Nathaniel. John and his brother journeyed out to western Pennsylvania when they were in their early twenties.

NARRATOR 2: One day, after working from break of day till the early evening, John Chapman and his brother were sitting by the side of the river just watching the sun go down behind the hills.

NATHANIEL: Sure is a fine day, John. We put in a good day's work . . . hard work . . . and everything is fine.

JOHN: Yes, indeed. It sure is a fine day! But, you know, I was just thinking that I'd like to do something else.

From *American Folklore, Legends, and Tall Tales for Readers Theatre* by Anthony D. Fredericks. Westport, CT: Teacher Ideas Press. Copyright © 2008.

NATHANIEL: What's that?

JOHN: I'd like to help out people more than I do. You know, there's lots of people coming along this river. Lots of people headed out to the west. And they're tired and weary and hungry. It's a long road they have to travel, and I'd like to help them on their way.

NATHANIEL: Help them! How do you plan to help them, John Chapman?

JOHN: I think I'd like to be a missionary.

NATHANIEL: You're not a preacher, John Chapman. You ain't got no training to be a preacher man. How are you going to be a missionary without the proper training?

JOHN: Not just any kind of missionary, dear brother. I'm going to be an apple missionary.

NATHANIEL: A what?

JOHN: An apple missionary. You see, there's lots of folks heading out to settle the great frontier. They're trying to start a new life in a new land. The traveling's tough and the roads are rough, and it ain't an easy life. I figured I could help those folks a little by giving them something to look forward to.

NATHANIEL: But an apple missionary . . . .

JOHN: That's right, brother. I had this dream that the frontier was filled with apple orchards. Mile upon mile of apple orchards. As far as the eye could see.

NATHANIEL: And how are apple orchards going to help the folks crossing the great frontier?

JOHN: Well, if I gather me lots of apple seeds and plant them up and down the valleys and in and out of the hills, there will be plenty of apples for all the pioneers in their westward travels.

NARRATOR 1: And so the next day John Chapman began to gather apple seeds from all the cider mills in and around Pittsburgh, Pennsylvania. He dried them in the sun and packed them in a big leather sack that he slung over his back.

NARRATOR 2: He put apple seeds in his shirt pockets and apple seeds in his pants pockets. He carried small bags of apple seeds tied 'round his waist.

NARRATOR 1: He began walking all over Pennsylvania and Ohio. He walked up long hills and down steep valleys. He walked barefoot through far-reaching fields and through woods and forests.

NARRATOR 2: And everywhere he went, and to everyone he met, he handed out apple seeds.

JOHNNY APPLESEED: [to Amy] Good day, Miss.

AMY: Good day, sir.

JOHNNY APPLESEED: Would you like some apple seeds?

AMY: Why would I need apple seeds?

JOHNNY APPLESEED: To plant along the edges of the woods, to plant beside your home, to plant in wide open fields. By planting the seeds you can help those travelers who are headed westward. You can help provide them with food and nourishment.

AMY: That sounds like a fine idea. I'm sure the travelers comin' this way would like to see some apple trees. And I'm sure those same travelers would like some apples to eat to help them on their long journey.

JOHNNY APPLESEED: I'd appreciate it if you would plant some of these here seeds. I'll be doing the same everywhere I walk. I plan to walk all the valleys and hike all the hills, planting my apple seeds everywhere I go.

NARRATOR 1: Each year Johnny Appleseed walked many miles, planting his apple seeds. As he made his way across the land, he would clear a field in the wilderness and plant his seeds. Afterward, he would build a wooden fence around the area to protect it and then be on his way.

NARRATOR 2: Johnny never stayed in one place very long. He would plant his seeds or give them to other people to plant, then he'd be off down the road or around the next bend.

NARRATOR 1: He was a strange fellow, that Johnny Appleseed. He never cut his hair or shaved his beard. He wore whatever people gave him and ate whatever they shared. Most of the time he walked barefoot and most of the time he wore an empty pot on his head. Everybody knew when Johnny Appleseed was coming to town. He never did need no introduction.

NARRATOR 2: Sometimes Johnny would stop at a cabin and help out with some of the chores in exchange for a meal and a place to lay his head.

JIM: Howdy, friend. I reckon you must be Johnny Appleseed.

JOHNNY APPLESEED: That's right. Can I help you with any of your chores here on your spread?

JIM: I reckon. Seems like there's always a lot to do around here. There's water to haul, pigs to slop, fields to mow, and crops to tend to. Jus' ain't enough hours in the day to get it all done.

JOHNNY APPLESEED: Don't you fret none. I'll be glad to help you out for a while.

JIM: I'd be much obliged, friend. Perhaps you'd like to share our supper with us. And we'd be happy to have you stay in the barn as long as you like.

JOHNNY APPLESEED: I'd much appreciate that.

JIM: So, where you headed for?

JOHNNY APPLESEED: I'm off to the Ohio Valley to plant some more apple orchards. I've still got a lots of apples to plant and lots of people to meet.

JIM: It's a right fine thing that you're doin'. I know that people will appreciate all those apple orchards when they come into bloom. It's a right fine thing that you're doin'.

NARRATOR 1: Month after month and year after year, Johnny would trek through the wilderness, planting his seeds and tending the many orchards that crisscrossed the great frontier. He was friendly to everybody—pioneers and Indians, and everybody else he met along the road.

NARRATOR 2: He was even kind to animals. It was said that he never harmed any animal. One time, I hear, a mean old hornet flew into his clothes. Johnny tried to shake the hornet out, but it just commenced to sting him time after time. Johnny kept shaking and shaking until the critter just got tired and flew away. When someone asked him why he didn't just kill the hornet, Johnny told him that that critter, as much as he was hurting him, had as much of a right to live as any other animal. And, besides, it just wasn't right to kill a living thing.

NARRATOR 1: There was another time when he was sitting around a campfire cooking up some beans. A bunch of bugs were attracted by the light and flew into the flames. Rather than seeing them harmed, Johnny put out the campfire and prevented any danger from befalling those bugs.

NARRATOR 2: Johnny Appleseed walked the land and planted all his trees for almost 50 years. He became a familiar figure along the roads that were etched into the countryside and beside the many rivers and streams in this new land. And he could always be found sharing his seeds and planting his beloved apple trees wherever he went. Even today, if you drive through Indiana, Ohio, and Pennsylvania, you can still see row after row of apple trees stretching out to the horizon . . . apple trees that probably came from Johnny Appleseed—an American legend.

Sweet Betsy from Pike

STAGING: The chorus may consist of two to four members. Each should be seated on a tall stool or chair with a copy of the script in his or her hands. The two main characters should be standing in the center of the staging area. They should pretend they are walking along a dusty trail somewhere in the West. The narrator should be positioned to one side of the staging area.

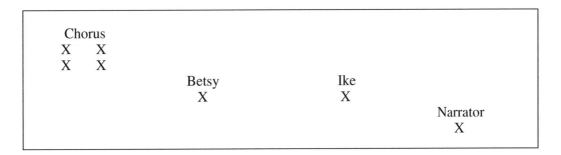

NARRATOR: It was sometime around 1850 when Sweet Betsy and her lover Ike set out from Missouri to seek their fortune in the gold fields of California. They set out with a wagon train full of other adventurers who were also seeking their fortunes. They all knew the journey would be long and arduous and that there would be much danger along the way. But they all wanted a better life—something none of them had ever had back in the Midwest.

CHORUS: Oh, don't you remember Sweet Betsy from Pike,
Who crossed the wide prairie with her lover Ike,
With two yoke of oxen, a big yellow dog,
A tall Shanghai rooster, and one spotted hog?

NARRATOR: They set out one day in the early spring. The sun was high and a long road lay before them. They traveled on a trail that had been cut by others who had come this way before them. There was a set of wagon wheel tracks before them—leading all the way to the wide, wide West. One evening they came to the Platte River. There before them lay a wide, green meadow. They were all tired because they had

From *American Folklore, Legends, and Tall Tales for Readers Theatre* by Anthony D. Fredericks. Westport, CT: Teacher Ideas Press. Copyright © 2008.

been traveling many days and most of them were not used to this form of travel. Betsy decided to lie down on the grass. She removed her shoes, lay on her back, and gazed up at the stars.

CHORUS: One evening quite early they camped on the Platte,
'Twas near by the road on a green shady flat.
Where Betsy, sore-footed, lay down to repose;
With wonder Ike gazed on that Pike County rose.

NARRATOR: Life on the trail was difficult. There were heat to deal with, animals to feed, miles to walk, camp to set up, illness and death at every bend. It was not an easy way to travel. Some turned back, but most people just kept slogging along—one step at a time—one step closer to their dream of a better life, a richer life, a life much better than they had ever known. But still, there were the daily troubles that seemed to be everywhere.

CHORUS: The Shanghai ran off, and their cattle all died;
That morning the last piece of bacon was fried.
Poor Ike was discouraged and Betsy got mad;
The dog drooped his tail and looked wondrously sad.

NARRATOR: Crossing the plains must have seemed easy to the pioneers when they came to the edge of the desert. The desert was a vast expanse that none of them had ever seen before, none of them had ever experienced before. It was dry, it was hot, and it was never-ending. Worst of all, there was little or no water to be found anywhere.

BETSY: I can't do it, Ike. I just can't do it. It's this desert. There's no water. There's no water anywhere. The sun is so hot. It blinds me anytime I look up. I just can't stand it any more. I just can't take it any more.

IKE: Betsy, my sweet Betsy. You have to go on. You have to keep moving. We don't want to die here in the desert. We don't want to give up before we even get to California. We must keep going. We must keep walking.

CHORUS: They soon reached the desert where Betsy gave out,
And down in the sand she lay rolling about,
While Ike, half distracted, looked on with surprise,
Saying . . .

IKE: Betsy, get up, you'll get sand in your eyes.

CHORUS: Sweet Betsy got up in a great deal of pain,
Declared . . .

BETSY: I'll go back to Pike County again;

CHORUS: But Ike gave a sigh and they fondly embraced,
And they traveled along with his arm round her waist.

NARRATOR: Besides the heat and the lack of water, there was another danger that the pioneers faced as they crossed the Wild West: Indians. Most of the people in the wagon train had never seen Indians before, but many had heard stories about how they posed a constant danger to any and all wagon trains that crossed their territory. This wagon train was no different!

CHORUS: The Injuns came down in a wild yelling horde,
And Betsy was scared they would scalp her adored.
Behind the front wagon wheel Betsy did crawl,
And there fought the Injuns with musket and ball.

The terrible desert was burning and bare, And Isaac he shrank from the death lurkin' there.

IKE: Dear old Pike County, I'll come back to you.

BETSY: Listen here, you'll go by yourself if you do.

NARRATOR: The journey was long, dangerous, and filled with many uncertainties. Lots of people died along the way, and lots never made it to the "promised land." But many did. Many realized their dreams and were able to make it all the way to California. Some

37

settled in the Sacramento Valley. Others kept going to the big city of San Francisco. Others swung northward and the lush green hills of Oregon.

CHORUS: They suddenly stopped on a very high hill,
With wonder looked down upon old Placerville.
Ike sighed when he said, and he cast his eyes down . . .

IKE: Sweet Betsy, my darling, we've got to Hangtown.

NARRATOR: But life in the West wasn't all hardship and pain. There were good times to be had as well. For most people those good times meant a dance at the town hall or out in the middle of the prairie. The music was loud, the punch was delicious, and the laughter was hearty. The tough times on the trail were usually forgotten—at least for a little while—as people danced across a wooden floor or under the blazing stars.

CHORUS: Long Ike and Sweet Betsy attended a dance.
Ike wore a pair of his Pike County pants.
Sweet Betsy was dressed up in ribbons and rings . . .

IKE: Sweet love, you're an angel, but where are your wings?

NARRATOR: It was a tough life. It was not a life for everyone. It usually took four or five months to get from Missouri to California. There were rivers to ford, mountains to climb, Indians to watch out for, diseases to fight, and death at every turn. But these pioneers kept coming. They helped to settle the West. They helped to claim a new land. They helped build the country. They were all heroes and heroines.

CHORUS: They swam wild rivers and climbed the tall peaks,
And camped on the prairies for weeks upon weeks.
Starvation and cholera, hard work and slaughter,
They reached Californy, 'spite of hell and high water.

CHAPTER 4

Tall Tales and Large Lies

Fibs. Lies. Untruths. Fabrications. Falsehoods. What do all those words have in common? They are uniquely and completely American. That is to say, Americans love a good story. And the more far-fetched or imaginative it is, the better! Impossible anecdotes and tall tales have been a part of the American storytelling experience ever since the first campfire was lit and the first lie was told. To make a story larger than life or stranger than truth must surely be the sine qua non of American storytelling.

Tall tales and wild yarns have sprung up all across the American landscape. From the shores of New England all the way to the gold fields of California, wild and imaginative stories have been part and parcel of the American experience. We have created oversized individuals, improbable experiences, and unimaginable situations to celebrate our creative spirit and relentless sense of (storytelling) adventure. These tales are classics in their own right; but equally important, they are representations of the landscape and imagination of the American people.

PAUL BUNYAN

A lumberman's life was often a solitary one. He might bunk down with a few fellers and eat his supper with a few more, but for the most part it was a life of peace and solitude. For that reason, lumbermen would create stories of the great American frontier. They would invent larger than life characters who would embody the best in every lumberman. Paul Bunyan was just one of those characters. Paul Bunyan was "born" in 1910 in a newspaper story written by James MacGillivray. In

1916 a lumberman named W. B. Laughead published a pamphlet of Paul Bunyan stories. Since then, entire collections of Paul Bunyan tall tales have been created for adults and children alike.

THE SAGA OF PECOS BILL

Pecos Bill originated from the pen of Edward O'Reilly. The first Pecos Bill story appeared in a 1923 issue of *Century Magazine*. O'Reilly captured the spirit, lustiness, and brazenness of the old West in a series of Western folklore tales that embodied comic tall-tale elements of Paul Bunyan, Davy Crockett, and Febold Feboldson. Other authors crafted additional stories about this classic Western character who became "the greatest cowpuncher ever known on either side of the Rockies, from Texas through Montana and on into Canada."

STORMALONG

Sailors are known for creating characters and tales that are both imaginative and creative. Stormalong is no different. His story sprang from the ports of New England in the days when enormous sailing ships plied the waters of the Atlantic, shipping goods or capturing whales to share with people all over the world. Stormalong was part of an old sea shanty that was sung whenever a ship weighed anchor. In 1930 stories about Stormalong were collected by Frank Shay, and later by C. E. Brown, into a collection that celebrates and underscores the life of a sailor—a life that is slowly fading into the past with the advent of supertankers and enormous cargo ships.

RIP VAN WINKLE

Surely one of the most well-known American literary characters is Rip Van Winkle. Rip was the creation of Washington Irving, who lived in the Hudson River valley of New York. That part of the country was originally settled by the Dutch, who brought with them a unique collection of ancestral stories. As a young boy, Irving listened to and thoroughly enjoyed these tales and superstitions. Later he began retelling and adapting them for American audiences. Rip Van Winkle became one of his best-known and most well-loved characters—if only because of the infamous 20-year nap.

FEBOLD FEBOLDSON

Febold Feboldson sprang from the heartland of the Great Plains. This section of the country presented farmers with many unique challenges, from the dangers of natural disasters to variations in soil. Farmers had to create and invent new ways of farming in order to survive. In 1923 Febold Feboldson was created by a Nebraska lumber dealer named Wayne Carroll to show the world how inventive and creative farmers could be. In 1937 Paul Beath collected a number of Febold Feboldson tales into a series of pamphlets that were distributed throughout the country. Febold's legacy, and his inventiveness, live on.

Paul Bunyan

STAGING: All five characters should be seated in a row across the staging area. Each may sit on a tall stool or high chair. Each may have a music stand in front of himself or herself. You may wish to tie a scarf around the neck of each character or invite the players to wear plaid shirts or old hats. You may wish to "build" a "fire" in the center of the staging area (red and orange construction paper cut into the shape of flames, each piece taped to a small log or piece of wood). (There is no narrator in this story.)

Logger 1	Logger 2	Logger 3	Logger 4	Logger 5
X	X	X	X	X

[campfire]

LOGGER 1: Well, my friends, here we are again, sitting around the campfire after a long day of cutting down all those trees in the forest. Whew! It sure was a hard day today. I can't believe how much work we were able to get done.

LOGGER 2: Work! Work!! Work!!! Why, what we did today was nothing. We just passed the time away, my friend. Heck, back in the good old days—well, that was when real work was done. Real work, my friend.

LOGGER 3: Yeah, that's when Paul Bunyan was around. Yeah, good old Paul Bunyan, the strongest and biggest lumberjack there ever was.

LOGGER 1: Well, tell me about him. What kind of fella was he?

LOGGER 4: Well, you see, Paul was born up in Maine. When he was just two weeks old he already weighed in at 100 pounds. Seems like he was growing faster than his parents could feed him. Why, just for breakfast he would have six dozen eggs, ten sacks of potatoes, and a half barrel of mush. It took a whole herd of

From *American Folklore, Legends, and Tall Tales for Readers Theatre* by Anthony D. Fredericks. Westport, CT: Teacher Ideas Press. Copyright © 2008.

cows just to supply him with the milk he drank at breakfast.

LOGGER 5: But that wasn't the strangest part. Nope. He had a beard—yup, Paul Bunyan even had a beard when he was a little baby. Why, his beard was so long and bushy that his mother had to comb it with a pine tree every two hours or so.

LOGGER 1: Wow, he sounds like he must have been some baby!

LOGGER 2: Yup, that he was. When he first learned to crawl he was nearly 500 pounds in weight. Why, when he crawled around the town he caused earthquakes so big that all the dishes in all the houses crashed down to the ground and the river spilled out of his banks.

LOGGER 3: When he took a nap, his parents put him in a sailing ship docked off the coast of Maine—hoping that the swells of the sea would rock him to sleep. But it seems that every time he rolled over huge waves crashed into the shore, causing all kinds of destruction.

LOGGER 4: Seems like the townspeople just got sick and tired of all the damage this giant baby was causing, and they commenced to ask Paul's parents if they would remove him from the town. So his parents began looking for some place that was big enough and wide enough and large enough for their baby.

LOGGER 1: What did they do?

LOGGER 5: Well, they sent him off to the North Woods—that part of the country we now call Minnesota, Michigan, and Wisconsin. It was an area filled to overflowing with trees . . . and lots and lots of space. Paul grew up fast in the North Woods.

LOGGER 2: But one winter it started to snow. It snowed and snowed and snowed. Most amazing was the fact that this wasn't just any snow—it was blue snow! Blanket upon blanket of blue snow covered the ground, covered the trees, covered the whole land.

LOGGER 3: One day Paul walked out into the snow, and he heard a something callin' from under the blue snow. It went, "Maa-maa." Paul looked all around, but couldn't see anything. "Maa-maa," he heard the sound again. He looked around again and saw a long tail sticking up out of the blue snow. When he pulled on the tail, out came the biggest baby ox on Earth. Except for a pair of white horns, the creature was a deep, deep blue all over its body.

LOGGER 4: Paul said, "Why, you're just a babe." And he slipped the ox into his shirt pocket and took it back to camp. When he got back he fed the blue ox a couple of barrels of milk and a couple of barrels of pancake mix. Now the ox (which Paul named "Babe") grew just as fast as a tornado twister. Why, each morning Babe would eat hundreds of pancakes.

LOGGER 5: Yeah, and if he didn't get enough pancakes he would go ahead and eat up all the plates. And he continued to grow—bigger and bigger each day. Why, it was said that it took 42 ax handles to measure the distance between his horns. It was also said that he weighed more than all the fish that ever got away. In fact, Babe grew to be so large that when he and Paul were walking through the woods, Babe's front end would be leaving Wisconsin just as his back end was entering it.

LOGGER 1: So, is that all there is?

LOGGER 2: Nope. There's much more to tell you. See, in those days the North Woods were covered with trees. And people were moving across the country to build new towns, new cities, and new factories all over the place. To build all that stuff, they needed trees. And the North Woods were just covered with trees. So Paul decided he would help out these pioneer folks and cut down some trees so that they could build their towns and cities.

LOGGER 3: That Paul Bunyan was not only big, he was smart, too. He figured that cutting down one tree at a time wasn't a very efficient way to get the lumber needed for all those houses. So, Paul invented the two-handled saw. Now this saw was more than a mile long. Paul stood at one end holding a handle, and a hundred men stood at the other end holding the other handle. Each side took turns pulling the handle through the woods. In no time at all they could cut down an entire forest.

LOGGER 4: But then they had to get all those logs down to the sawmill so they could be cut into boards. The best way to do that was to float them down the river. But they had just one problem with the river.

LOGGER 1: What's that?

LOGGER 5: Well, you see, that river had so many twists and turns that the logs would all get bunched up at the bends in the river.

LOGGER 1: So what happened?

LOGGER 2: Well, Paul just hitched up Babe the blue ox to one end of the river. Babe commenced to pull as hard as he could on the river and before too long that river was all straightened out. Then Paul and his men could send those logs down the river without having them get caught on any bends or curves.

LOGGER 3: Paul had so many men working for him that he had to build a high-rise bunkhouse for them all to sleep in. Why, that bunkhouse was so tall that the top 17 stories had a hinge on them so that they could let the moon pass by in the middle of the night.

LOGGER 4: To get to the top bunks, Paul sent his men up in hot-air balloons. And when they wanted to come down to breakfast in the morning, they had to each strap on a parachute and jump.

44

LOGGER 5: Yeah, and those were some breakfasts that they ate. Why, each lumberjack could eat about 100 pancakes, drink 50 cups of coffee, and consume 10 football fields of cornbread every morning.

LOGGER 2: The batter for the pancakes had to be mixed in a concrete mixer, which was something that Paul invented all by himself. The skillet was so big that it took 25 men with slabs of bacon tied to their feet to grease it.

LOGGER 3: One time, Paul and his crew were logging somewhere in the Midwest. Paul wanted to try out some new food to feed his men. So he discovered a new kind of corn, which sprang up six feet just overnight.

LOGGER 4: Yeah, and that corn grew a foot a minute all the next day. It was growing so fast that Paul decided that he should get it to stop. So he sent one of his men to climb the cornstalk. But the stalk grew faster than the man could climb it. Soon the man and the top of the corn stalk disappeared into the clouds. It was getting near about supper time, so Paul had to fill his rifle with biscuits and fire them up to the man so that he wouldn't starve.

LOGGER 5: Well, after a couple of days the top of that cornstalk grew just a little too close to the sun. Around noontime all that corn started popping, and a blizzard of popcorn covered the countryside. Unfortunately, a herd of cows somewhere in Kansas thought that the popcorn was a real blizzard, and they all froze to death. Eventually the cornstalk stopped growing and the blizzard was over.

LOGGER 1: Wow! That Paul Bunyan character sure got himself into a lot of interesting stories.

LOGGER 2: That's not all! You see, after the popcorn blizzard in Kansas, Paul and Babe headed off for Arizona for a little vacation. It was a long way there, and Paul got a little tired. He began to drag his big ax on the ground behind him as he was walking. He didn't realize what he was doing until it was too late. By the time he realized what he had done, he had created the Grand Canyon. Lots of people visit the Grand Canyon today just to see how Paul created it with his big ax.

LOGGER 3: When Paul got back to the North Woods it was winter again. His men were out in the woods cutting down all the trees that they could. But this wasn't just any winter. This was the year of the Hard Winter. This was the year that the air was so cold that when people spoke their words froze in the air.

LOGGER 4: Yeah, they would have to wait around till spring just so those words would thaw out and they could hear what was said in the winter time. Why, I hear that there are still some words frozen up in the North Woods that haven't been heard for 50 years or more. No telling what was said, but it might be some time before anybody knows.

LOGGER 1: My, my, my! That Paul Bunyan sure sounds like one amazing fella!

LOGGER 5: Well, that might be true. But I don't think he is any more amazing than all of us right here!

The Saga of Pecos Bill

STAGING: The four narrators should all be seated on stools or high chairs. They should each have their scripts on a music stand or lectern. The other characters (some of whom only have a few lines) may be standing or walking around the staging area.

```
Narrator 1        Narrator 2        Narrator 3        Narrator 4
   X                 X                 X                 X

      Pecos Bill      Pa        Ma
         X            X         X

         Cowboy 1              Mountain Lion          Cowboy 2
            X                       X                    X
```

NARRATOR 1: Now as you all know, Texas is a pretty big state. In fact, it's the biggest state of them all. And 'cause it's such a big state, it has big heroes. And the biggest of all the heroes was Pecos Bill, the King of the Cowboys.

NARRATOR 2: You see, Pecos Bill wasn't originally from Texas. No sir. He was from somewhere back east. From a family of 15 or 20 kids. In fact, there were so many kids in the family that the parents just didn't remember all the names of all the children.

NARRATOR 3: Well, as I heard it, Bill wanted a teddy bear—just like any other kid. But 'cause his family was so poor they couldn't afford a teddy bear just for Bill. So he decided to go out and get his own. So one day he crawled out of his crib and into the woods. There he found a genuine grizzly bear, which he wrapped up in his arms and took on home. Seems like Bill was going to be a little different from everyone else.

NARRATOR 4: One day Bill's parents heard about some new land in the West. They heard that there was plenty of land . . . plenty of land for families with 15 or 20 children.

From *American Folklore, Legends, and Tall Tales for Readers Theatre* by Anthony D. Fredericks. Westport, CT: Teacher Ideas Press. Copyright © 2008.

PA: Hey, Ma, I hear that there's plenty of land in the West for families with lots of children.

MA: You mean families like ours with so many children that we just can't remember all their names.

PA: Yup!

MA: Well, why don't we just up and move out to that there West so we can build us a house big enough for all these children?

PA: Sounds like a grand idea!

NARRATOR 1: And so Pa and Ma packed all their children and all their animals in the back of their wagon and headed out for the West.

NARRATOR 2: However, as soon as the wagon went over the state line between Arkansas and Texas it bounced Bill clean out of the wagon and alongside the road.

NARRATOR 3: Since there were so many children and animals in the wagon, nobody noticed that Bill wasn't in the wagon until about a week later. By then it was too late to go look for him, but Bill's parents figured that any baby who could wrestle a grizzly bear was certainly tough enough to survive in the wilds of Texas.

NARRATOR 4: As it happens, Bill got along fine. After falling out of the wagon, he crawled into a cave of coyotes and fell asleep. The mama coyote took a liking to Bill and began to raise him as her own. Bill soon learned all the ways of coyote life. He learned how to bay at the moon, how to hunt rabbits, and how to wrestle with all the other coyotes in the den. Pretty soon, Bill was just a regular coyote.

NARRATOR 1: One day Bill was lapping up some water from the Pecos River along with the other coyotes. That's when a cowboy spotted him.

COWBOY 1: What in tarnation! You're just lapping up that water like you was a regular coyote.

PECOS BILL: Well, that's what I am—a coyote. Anyways, ain't you never seen a real coyote afore?

COWBOY 1: 'Course I have. But you're not like any coyote I've ever seen. You look more like a human than you do a coyote.

PECOS BILL: But I am a coyote. I have fleas just like a coyote, don't I?

COWBOY 1: Lots of people in Texas have fleas. That don't mean nothin'. The thing that all coyotes got is a tail.

NARRATOR 2: With that, Bill turned around and looked at his rear end. It was then, for the first time in his life, that he realized he didn't have a tail.

PECOS BILL: Dang it all. I don't have a tail like my brothers and sisters. But if I'm not a coyote, then what am I?

COWBOY 1: You're a human being.

NARRATOR 3: Pecos Bill began to growl just like his coyote mother had taught him. But he knew deep down in his heart that he wasn't a real coyote. So he figured he might as well go along with the cowboy and begin acting like a real human acts.

NARRATOR 4: Bill started walking alongside the cowboy. They hadn't gone very far when a huge mountain lion jumped down from a cliff and right onto Bill's back. Without ever having to think about it, Bill just up and wrestled that mountain lion to the ground as quick as you please.

BILL: You give up, you varmint?

MOUNTAIN LION: Yes, I give up.

BILL: Now, I reckon that your huntin' days are over. Seeing as how I need to be more like a human and less like a coyote, I guess I'm just going to have to use you like a horse.

MOUNTAIN LION: A horse!

BILL: Yep, a horse!

MOUNTAIN LION: You going to put a saddle on me?

BILL: Nope. I'm just going' to ride you like a horse. So let's be on our way.

NARRATOR 1: Bill jumped on the back of the mountain lion and he and the cowboy continued on their way.

NARRATOR 2: They hadn't gone but 10 miles when a 10-foot rattlesnake swung out of a cactus plant and down on top of them.

NARRATOR 3: Bill jumped off the mountain lion's back and grabbed the end of that snake. He swung that snake around and around his head. As the snake was spinning round and round, it grew thinner and thinner. It also got longer and longer. By the time Bill was done, that 10-foot rattlesnake was 30 feet long.

NARRATOR 4: Bill coiled up that 30-foot snake just like it was a rope and slung it over his shoulder. From then on cowboys always carried a rope with them just like Pecos Bill carried a 30-foot snake with him wherever he went.

NARRATOR 1: After that, Bill and the cowboy rode on until they got to the ranch alongside the Pecos River. The other cowboys didn't know what to make of Bill, riding his mountain lion and carrying a snake wrapped across his shoulders. But I guess they could see that he was a good man, so they figured he'd be a good cowboy, too.

PECOS BILL: Howdy, folks, I'm new in these here parts. I just want to learn how to be a cowboy and help you fellas out.

COWBOY 2: Well, friend, you're welcome to stay as long as you want. We're always looking for new help, seeing as we have the whole state of Texas to take care of and lots of cattle to keep an eye on.

50

PECOS BILL: I appreciate that. By the way, what would you like to have me do now?

COWBOY 2: Well, I don't think it's anything you can help us with. See, we're just in the biggest drought that Texas ever had. We ain't had no water for months and months now.

PECOS BILL: Well, I reckon I can help with that.

NARRATOR 2: And with that, Bill just swung his rattlesnake lasso round and round and he roped up all the water from the Rio Grande River. After that there was no more problem with any drought.

NARRATOR 3: Seems like there was nothing that Bill couldn't do. Like that one time when the biggest and meanest tornado that ever was came into Texas. Bill decided that the only way to tame that tornado was to ride it until it spun itself out.

NARRATOR 4: So Bill just waited until that tornado came up and over the state line with Oklahoma. It slowed down a little as it crossed into Texas, and that's when Bill just up and jumped on that tornado's back.

NARRATOR 1: Now, that tornado didn't like anybody ridin' its back. It turned itself from green to brown to black and began to leaping around like it was full of about a hundred wildcats. That tornado whipped and whirled and whipped and whirled some more, just tryin' to throw Bill off its back.

PECOS BILL: Yowee! Hold on tight! I aim to tame you, seein' as how I'm the toughest cowboy in these here parts. You ain't about to throw me. No sir.

NARRATOR 2: Well, that tornado started to cuss and swear and do all kinds of mean things as it spun faster and faster. It humped its back, it threw itself all about, it jumped up and it jumped down, trying to toss Bill back on to the ground. It just got meaner and meaner every way it twisted and turned.

NARRATOR 3: In fact, it got to be so mean and so ornery that it tied up rivers into knots and emptied lakes of all their water. Why, Bill and that twister went from one end of Texas to the other—the twister was twisting and Bill was hangin' on for dear life. But try as it might that twister could never throw Bill. No way! Bill just rode that tornado like it was the meanest bull at a rodeo. He jabbed it with his spurs and wrapped his arms tighter and tighter around that spinning tornado.

NARRATOR 4: Finally, that tornado figured it wasn't going to get Bill off its back. So it headed itself out to California and just rained itself out. Seems it rained so much water that it washed out the Grand Canyon. Why, that mean old tornado was worn down to nothing, and by the time they both reached the Pacific Ocean, that tornado was nothing but a little bitty puff of wind.

NARRATOR 1: When Bill fell off, he hit the ground so hard that the ground just sank right below sea level. Folks in those parts now call that part of California Death Valley.

PECOS BILL: There, that should teach those tornadoes a thing or two!

NARRATOR 2: When Bill got back to Texas, he started to clean up the mess he and that tornado had made.

NARRATOR 3: When he first climbed on the back of the tornado, Texas had been covered by forests of trees. But now all the land had been swept clean of every single tree from the full force of that wrestling match between Bill and the tornado.

NARRATOR 4: And if you go and visit Texas today, you will see lots of wide open spaces all over the state. Wide open spaces thanks to that wrestling match between the greatest cowboy who ever lived and one mean and wild tornado. Yup, Pecos Bill was the best cowboy there ever was . . . the meanest, the strongest, and the best there ever was!

Stormalong

STAGING: The characters may all walk around the staging area. They should each carry a copy of the script. If possible, provide Stormalong with a sailor's hat or place a small sailing ship on a table in the middle of the staging area.

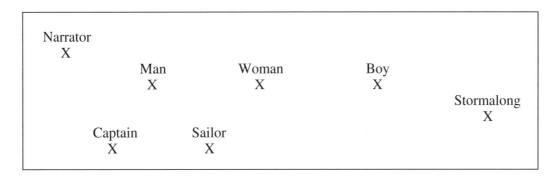

```
Narrator
   X
              Man          Woman          Boy
               X             X             X
                                                      Stormalong
                                                          X
         Captain      Sailor
            X           X
```

NARRATOR: Now, this here story that you're about to hear is a true one. Ain't no fiction here—this is as true as the hair on my head. Least it's as true as the folks of Cape Cod are . . . not that they've ever told a lie, 'specially when they've been out in the sun too long.

Anyway, seems along about 1800 or so there was this giant wave that up and roared over the Cape. When the water had receded the villagers went out and began to hear a sound, a wailing, coming from the beach. When they went down there they found a baby who was three fathoms tall. Now, for those of you who ain't been born to the sea, that's about 18 feet. And that enormous baby was wailing something terrible.

Well, the townsfolk hauled that great big baby into a wheelbarrow and carried him back into town. They fed him barrels of milk and buckets of porridge.

WOMAN: What will we name him?

MAN: Don't know that there would be a proper name for a baby this big.

BOY: How 'bout Alfred Bulltop Stormalong? We could call him "Stormy" for short.

NARRATOR: The townspeople all cheered. And at that, the 18-foot-tall baby let out a burp so loud that it just about blew off the roof of the town hall.

The town adopted Stormalong, and everyone pitched in to raise the giant baby. Now as you might imagine, Stormy was always the center of attention, seein' as he was the biggest thing that town ever saw. But Stormy never did like all that attention, so after school each day he would slip on down to the beach, swim out to the deepest part of the ocean, and ride the whales just for fun. Stormy, ever since he was a young tyke, sure did love the ocean. In fact, folks around these here parts used to say that Stormy had saltwater in his veins.

By the time Stormy was 12 years old he was already six fathoms tall. That's about 36 feet in height.

WOMAN: Stormy, we all love you, but your gettin' just a mite too large for this town.

MAN: Yeah! There ain't a building in this town that's big enough to hold you. Why, you're even larger than the steeple on the church.

BOY: I guess you're going to have to go somewhere else—somewhere that's big enough to hold you.

NARRATOR: Stormy glanced behind him and saw the wide expanse of the ocean. He knew that there was only one place in the world that was large enough to keep him. So he hoisted his trunk up over his shoulder and set off for Boston—where all the sailing ships were.

STORMALONG: Yep, a sailor's life is the only life for me. A whole ocean is the only place that's large enough to keep me happy. So I guess I'm on my way to seek my fortune on the sea.

NARRATOR: When Stormalong got to Boston he asked where the biggest ship on the sea was docked. Everyone said that there was only one ship that fit that description—*The Lady of the Sea.*

CAPTAIN: Well, shiver me timbers, I ain't never seen a man as tall or as big as you are, sailor.

STORMALONG: Well, you might be right about my size, but just so's you know, I ain't a man yet. I'm just 12 years old, and I'm out to seek my fortune among the saltwater and waves.

SAILOR: Well, blow me down. I guess you're going to be about the biggest cabin boy there ever was. Come on aboard and stow your gear. We're just about ready to hoist the anchor and set sail for South America.

NARRATOR: When all the other sailors first saw Stormalong, they just couldn't believe their eyes. They'd never seen a person as large or as big as Stormalong. But pretty soon they just got used to him, seein' as how he could do the work of any three men put together.

CAPTAIN: He's sure a good one to have on board. Pitches in and does all his work. He's a good one, that's for sure.

SAILOR: A good friend, too. He ain't never let a man down.

NARRATOR: The *Lady of the Sea* set was on its way to South America—one of the best places in the world to find whales—for *The Lady* was a whaling ship of great reputation. It always came back to port filled to the bridge with whale blubber. The captain knew how to find whales, and the crew knew how to capture them.

One day, after spending some time off the coast of Argentina, the captain gave the order to hoist the anchor.

CAPTAIN: Hoist the anchor, me laddies. We're off to new territory. We're off for more whales.

55

NARRATOR: But when the crew tried to pull up the anchor, nothin' happened.

SAILOR: We pulled and we pulled, and that anchor jus' doesn't want to come up. Seems like there's something down below holdin' on to it.

NARRATOR: The lookout peered over the edge, and sure as you might, he saw a giant octopus holding on to that anchor—holding on to the anchor with half of his tentacles and holding on to seaweed on the ocean floor with the other half of his tentacles. Seems as though that giant octopus wasn't going to let go of that anchor no matter how hard the sailors pulled on the line.

STORMALONG: Ain't no bother. I'll go and take care o' that little fishy!

CAPTAIN: That ain't no fishy, Stormalong. That there is one giant octopus. Not only that, it's a giant octopus that aims to stay around a long time.

STORMALONG: Ain't no bother, Captain. I can take care of it.

NARRATOR: Stormy stuck a knife between his teeth, climbed out onto the bowsprit, and dove into the foaming water.

SAILOR: Now, what's he done? He ain't no match for that there monster.

NARRATOR: The water boiled with fury and terrible sounds came from beneath the waves. The ship began to pitch from side to side—rockin' and rollin' back and forth in the boiling waters. It seemed like the whole ocean was jus' going to swallow up *The Lady*.

Well, the ocean sloshed back and forth for a good part of a hour. It looked as though the ship and everybody on it was going to be sent to a watery grave, when suddenly the water grew calm again. Stormy's head soon bobbed to the surface. Someone called out to throw him a line, but before one could be brought forward, Stormy had grabbed the anchor chain and climbed hand over hand onto the deck. Once aboard he hauled up the anchor chain and the ship once again began to cut through the sea.

CAPTAIN: What happened?

STORMALONG: Oh, just a little disagreement with an eight-armed varmint.

SAILOR: You mean a fight with a two-ton octopus.

STORMALONG: Well, I guess you're right.

CAPTAIN: So, what did you do?

STORMALONG: Well, he didn't want to let go of our anchor. So I just wrestled his eight tentacles into a whole bunch of double knots. I reckon' it'll take him a month o' Sundays 'fore he'll ever get all those knots untied.

NARRATOR: And so the legend of Alfred Bulltop Stormalong began. His reputation spread up and down the Atlantic seaboard, and soon every sailor there was wanted to sail with Stormy. He became one of the most admired of all the sailors that ever set their feet on a whaling ship. Yep, Alfred Bulltop Stormalong was one unbelievable sailor!

Rip Van Winkle

STAGING: There are two "sets" of characters—those who come before Rip Van Winkle's "sleep" and those who come afterward. Each "set" should be standing at music stands or lecterns.

```
Narrator
X

            Rip Van Winkle              Wife
                  X                       X
                        Stranger
                           X        Old Man      Old Woman
                                       X             X
_____

Narrator
X

            Rip Van Winkle
                  X
      Child 1              Child 2
         X                   X
                                     Mayor        Woman
                                       X            X
```

NARRATOR: Once upon a long time ago, way up in the Catskill Mountains of New York, there lived a fine man by the name of Rip Van Winkle. He was a hard worker, but he also loved to roam the beautiful mountains with his trusty dog and hunt for squirrels.

WIFE: Rip, where you be going this fine morning?

RIP VAN WINKLE: Well, woman, I reckon I'll be traveling down the road to see if I can fetch us some squirrel meat for the table.

WIFE: Now that would be fine. Seems like we ain't had any meat since a month of Sundays, and I aim to fix us a fine Sunday supper with all the trimmin's.

From *American Folklore, Legends, and Tall Tales for Readers Theatre* by Anthony D. Fredericks. Westport, CT: Teacher Ideas Press. Copyright © 2008.

RIP VAN WINKLE: Well, then, Hound Dog and I better be gettin' on our way. It's a fine day, and I don't want to be wastin' any of it.

WIFE: You be careful now. Watch where you go and be sure to be home afore the sun goes down.

RIP VAN WINKLE: I will, woman. I'll be off now.

NARRATOR: Rip set off down the dusty road and up into the mountains. He had been traveling for some time—with nary a sight of a squirrel—when he decided it might be a good thing to set a spell and rest his weary bones. His dog lay down beside him, and as he looked out across the mountains he could see green slopes and wide valleys all around him. Then from out of nowhere he heard a voice calling his name.

STRANGER: Rip. Rip. Rip Van Winkle.

RIP VAN WINKLE: Who goes there?

STRANGER: It is only I.

NARRATOR: As Rip looked down the trail he could see a strange figure approaching him. His dog gave a low growl, but the stranger did not appear to be frightened. His pace was slow because he was burdened by a large pack on his back.

STRANGER: Greetings, friend. I bear a heavy weight and was wondering if you would be kind enough to help me with it.

RIP VAN WINKLE: Of course. Where are you headed for?

STRANGER: Just up the valley here. If you could just help me haul this cask, I would be mighty grateful.

RIP VAN WINKLE: What is in this here cask?

STRANGER: Oh, just some of the finest mead in all these parts. Help me out, and I would sure be glad to share a pint or two.

NARRATOR: Rip grabbed one end of the cask while the stranger grabbed the other. They passed through a ravine, along the edge of a crystal clear stream, and up an old trail cut into the side of the mountain. Rip had lived in the mountains all his life, but he was not familiar with this trail. Soon they entered a small village, one that was quite unfamiliar to Rip. There in the center of the village was a group of people playing at a game of ninepins.

OLD MAN: What brings you here, stranger?

RIP VAN WINKLE: I was just helping your friend here bring this fine cask of mead to the village.

OLD WOMAN: We be mighty grateful for your help. You're welcome to stay a spell and rest your tired bones.

RIP VAN WINKLE: I thank you, Old Woman. But I ain't never seen nor heard of this village, and I've been livin' in these hills all my life.

OLD WOMAN: Oh, we been here for a long time. Can't remember how long, but that don't matter. We're just good folks who like to have a good time.

NARRATOR: At that a loud rumble shook the village, and Rip realized that someone had rolled his ball right through the ninepins for a good score. The rumbling echoed across the valley for a time and then vanished.

OLD MAN: Grab yourself a pint from the cask and set a spell.

RIP VAN WINKLE: Thanks, I believe I will.

NARRATOR: Rip sat under a tree and drank an entire flagon of mead. It was some of the finest drink he had ever had, and he decided to have another. By the time he was near the bottom of his third drink, his eyes had grown heavy and his senses were overpowered. His eyes swam in his head, and his head slowly lowered to his chest. In minutes he fell into a deep and powerful sleep.

60

[At this point all the previous characters, with the exception of Rip, should exit the staging area. Their places should be taken by the new set of characters.]

NARRATOR: Rip slowly woke up from his sleep. He found himself on the same green knoll where he had drunk the fine and delicious mead. He rubbed his eyes and began to look around him. He began to recall the experiences before his sleep—the stranger with the cask, the townspeople in the village, the game of ninepins, and the fine and tasty mead.

RIP VAN WINKLE: Well, ain't this fine. I've gone and fallen asleep, and now everybody's departed. I wonder where they went.

NARRATOR: Rip looked for his gun, but all that was beside him was a rusty old firelock. He suspected that his fine oiled rifle had been stolen while he slept. He called for his dog, but there was not a sound to be heard from the hound anywhere. He decided it was late and that he had better return to his home and his wife. As he approached his own village he met a number of people—but none that he recognized. They all looked at him with surprise in their eyes. It was then that he discovered that his beard was now over two feet in length and that his hair cascaded down over his shoulders. As he looked around, he did not recognize any of the houses, and when he turned the corner toward his favorite inn he saw nothing more than an old abandoned building. He was confused. He could not find anything familiar.

CHILD 1: Hey, old man, where did you come from?

RIP VAN WINKLE: What do you mean? I come from right here. This is the village where I grew up. This is the village where I built my house. This is the village where my wife and I lived for many a year.

CHILD 2: Well, then, who are you?

RIP VAN WINKLE: I'm Rip Van Winkle.

CHILD 1: Rip Van Winkle! I don't know any Rip Van Winkle.

61

NARRATOR: Rip looked at the child with amazement. Then he realized that the child would have been too young to remember who he was. He was about to ask another question when a crowd of people began to gather around him. They were amazed at this stranger, and no one seemed to recognize him.

MAYOR: Greetings, friend. How may we help you?

RIP VAN WINKLE: My name's Rip Van Winkle, and this here is the town where I live. But I don't recognize anything. I don't seem to know anybody here. Where's Nicholas Vedder?

MAYOR: Hmm, Nicholas Vedder. Now, as I recall, good old Nicholas has been dead and gone a good 18 years now. There was a wooden tombstone in the churchyard that used to tell all about him, but that's rotten and gone too.

RIP VAN WINKLE: Where's Van Bummel, the schoolmaster?

MAYOR: He went off to the wars. Nobody's heard about him for well over 15 years now.

RIP VAN WINKLE: Does anybody here know Rip Van Winkle?

NARRATOR: There was a murmur in the crowd, but no one said anything. Finally a woman stepped out of the crowd and walked over to Rip.

WOMAN: Why, I once knew a Rip Van Winkle. He was a fine man and a fine husband for his wife.

RIP VAN WINKLE: How do you know this man?

WOMAN: Why, Rip Van Winkle was my father. But it's been 20 years since he went away from his home with his gun and his dog, and he's never been heard of since. His dog came home without him, but whether he was carried away by Indians or got lost in the mountains, nobody can tell. I was then but a little girl.

RIP VAN WINKLE: I . . . I am Rip Van Winkle. I am your father, Rip Van Winkle. Please tell me girl, where is your fine mother?

WOMAN: Oh, she died but a short time ago. She broke a blood vessel in her head and died quite suddenly. I am still saddened by her loss. But my sadness is now tempered by the arrival of my long lost father. My father, Rip Van Winkle, has returned and has re-entered my life. I am full of joy.

NARRATOR: And so it was that Rip finally returned to his village. He does not know, nor does he understand, why the 20 lost years seem as though they were but one night. But the neighbors still talk about it, wagging their tongues as if they know the reason why. And every summer when the thunderstorms rumble through the valley, Rip Van Winkle casts his eyes up the valley. He's not sure, but sometimes the rumbling of thunder sounds just like a game of ninepins being played in a far and distant village.

Febold Feboldson

STAGING: The characters should all be at lecterns or podiums. Febold Feboldson should be in the center of the staging area. If possible, dress "Febold" in coveralls or worn blue jeans and a farmer's hat.

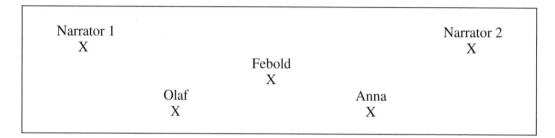

Narrator 1
X

Narrator 2
X

Febold
X

Olaf
X

Anna
X

NARRATOR 1: A long time ago—way out on the plains of this here great country—there lived a farmer by the name of Febold Feboldson. Now Febold wasn't your usual farmer. Febold was a farmer with ideas . . . lots of ideas . . . hundreds of ideas . . . yep, thousands of ideas. Why, you could say that Febold was the "Idea Farmer."

NARRATOR 2: That's right. See, Febold lived way out on the prairies . . . what you and I call the Great Plains. He was originally from Sweden, but he came over to this country 'cause he heard about all the land that was available and all the good crops that could be grown on all that land. Febold, being an adventurous type, decided to pack up his family and pack up his bags and head on over to this country of the United States.

NARRATOR 1: However, when Febold got to these here lands, he found that there was lots of lands and there was lots of crops that could be grown on those lands.

NARRATOR 2: But what he didn't find was lots of water. That's right, the Great Plains was rich in land, but poor in water. It was also just darn hot.

OLAF: Hey, it sure is hot around here. I jus' can't stand all this heat. Why, there's so much hot weather around these parts that I jus' can't get a crop to grow.

ANNA: Yup! It sure does get hot around here. Jus' seems as though everything around here is jus' plain hot. Can't even walk outside without getting' hot. Can't go nowhere without getting' hot. Seems like it's too hot to grow any crops around here, I reckon.

OLAF: Yup. My tongue's jus' hangin' out all the time. I reckon we should jus' up and pack our bags and move on out to California. I hear they have plenty of room, plenty of land, and plenty of rain for all those crops they grow.

ANNA: You're right, Olaf. I think we should jus' up and move on out to California.

FEBOLD: Now, jus' a moment, friends. Don't you be moving on out to California for no good reason. I can solve this here heat problem.

NARRATOR 1: Now, there's one thing that Febold was—he was a thinker. That's right—a thinker. In fact, he was one of the fastest thinkers there ever was. Before Olaf and Anna and all Febold's friends could climb up into their wagons and head on off to the West, he jumped up and yelled:

FEBOLD: WAIT! Stay here, my friends, and I promise you some rain!

OLAF: Some rain. Febold? Are you crazy? We ain't seen any rain for more than a month now, and we don't expect to see any rain for another month or so.

ANNA: We can't live like this. We can't grow our crops without any rain.

FEBOLD: But jus' wait and I can solve your problem in no time!

NARRATOR 2: So, Febold thought and he thought and he thought, until he came up with about a hundred ideas in just three seconds.

NARRATOR 1: But there was one idea that made him dance.

NARRATOR 2: Yup, that idea was to build a big bonfire right next to the lake jus' outside of town.

NARRATOR 1: So that's what he did. He built the biggest bonfire anyone had ever seen.

NARRATOR 2: That bonfire was so big and it burned so hot that soon all the water in the lake vaporized and formed a large bank of clouds over the prairie.

NARRATOR 1: The clouds were so big and so heavy that they began to crash into one another.

NARRATOR 2: Each time they crashed into one another, it rained. Lots and lots of rain! Buckets and buckets of rain! Barrels and barrels of rain! Yup, it jus' rained and rained and rained.

NARRATOR 1: Yup, all that rain! Except there was jus' one little problem. The problem was that none of the rain ever reached the ground.

NARRATOR 2: That was because the air was so hot and dry that the rain jus' turned to steam before it even got down to the ground.

OLAF: Hey, Febold. Will you look at that? You made it rain like crazy, but all that rain is jus' not reaching the ground.

ANNA: Yeah, we got all the rain we could ask for. It's jus' that we ain't got the rain to come down far enough to the ground to help the crops.

FEBOLD: Don't worry, my friends. I'll come up with a solution.

NARRATOR 1: So Febold thought and thought and thought, and he came up with about a thousand ideas in about three seconds. But there was one idea that was better than all the other ideas.

NARRATOR 2: Febold ran into his shed and came back with a big pair of clippers.

NARRATOR 1: All his friends watched as Febold took that big pair of clippers and began clipping the steam into long strips.

NARRATOR 2: He then took all those strips of steam and began to tuck them into the ground. He would take one strip and tuck it between a row of crops.

NARRATOR 1: Yup, then he would take another strip of steam and tuck it in between another row of crops.

NARRATOR 2: Pretty soon his friends realized what he was doing and they all began to do the same thing.

NARRATOR 1: It wasn't long before they had all the strips of steam tucked into the ground. And it wasn't too long after that that those rows of crops all began to grow now that they all had enough water tucked in between them.

OLAF: Febold, I must say, you got to be the best thinker there ever was. Why, there's no reason for us to go off to California. We can make enough water to put on our crops whenever we want to.

ANNA: Febold, I think that you jus' saved the day for us. You sure are one great thinker, you are. I reckon we'll jus' stay here a while and grow our crops jus' like we planned to do at the start.

NARRATOR 2: And so it was that Febold Feboldson saved the day for his friends and neighbors. And from that day forward, many other people came to the Great Plains to settle down. 'Cause they knew that with Febold around they would never run out of water.

NARRATOR 1: Jus' goes to show what a good thinker can do when he puts his mind to a problem.

NARRATOR 2: Yup. That's jus' what this country needed—a good thinker. And Febold Feboldson was jus' that sort of person!

CHAPTER 5

Rascals and Ruffians

The United States in the 1700s and 1800s contained a mix of characters unlike at any other time in our history. Some were good folks; some were not. Suffice it to say that the men and women who set out for the frontiers of this great land were a curious collection of ruffians, drinkers, brawlers, cutthroats, liars, cheaters, ladies, gentlemen, fakes, and fools. Each one, in his or her own special and unique way, made a contribution to the fabric of this country.

The stories that arose out of the exploits and adventures of these folks were steeped in imagination and creativity. One never knew how much truth was embedded in a tale or how much veracity was woven throughout a story that found its way back from the frontier and into everyday American life. Those were wild times, and the people who lived them were frequently as rough and tumble as the stories they wove for an audience—whether that audience was a traveling companion sitting by a campfire or a saloon full of strangers at the end of the road.

BRER RABBIT

Brer Rabbit can be traced back to the trickster tales that are part of the storytelling traditions of Central and Southern Africa. In many African cultures, the trickster is usually Anansi the Spider; however, there are many similarities between rabbit and spider tales. The American version of rabbit trickster tales is suggested by some to represent the black slave who uses his wits to overcome adversity and outsmart his enemies (most notably the white slave owners). Joel Chandler Harris initially collected these stories (principally in Georgia) in the late nineteenth century and put them into print for a mainstream audience.

MIKE FINK

Mike Fink was an actual keelboat man. He was born in the wilderness near Fort Pitt (in what is now Pennsylvania) in 1770. At an early age he developed a talent for sharpshooting and scouting. He found his true love, however, on the river. He became a celebrated keelboat man as well as a well-known fighter, brawler, drinker, and hard worker. His fame as a rough and tough individual spread far and, as is often the case, his legend grew. Many stories sprang up about some of Mike's exploits—some true, many false. But that was the nature of frontier life. It was often a mixture of fact and fiction—resulting in stories that were more imaginative than authentic.

"THAT'S ONCE!"

One of the endearing qualities about American folklore is the humor embedded in the stories and tales that have been passed down from one generation to another. This tale is a classic example of folklore humor. There is no single origin of the story, but most accounts put its beginnings in the Appalachian Mountain region of western Virginia. I have intentionally used a regional dialect to add some additional flavor to this retelling.

THE WIDOW AND THE ROBBERS

The old West was known for many things. But rarely was anything better known than some of the famous gunfighters of the day. Names like Doc Holliday, Billy the Kid, Black Bart, and Butch Cassidy were celebrated far and wide as some of the sharpest shooters there ever were. Stories, some true, most of them fictional, sprang up about these gunfighters and their exploits. Lives were lost and legends arose as these individuals made their fame (and sometimes their fortune) across the wild, wild West. Many met untimely ends, but their legends have frequently transcended their earthly exploits.

Brer Rabbit

STAGING: The two narrators should stand at lecterns on either side of the staging area. The other characters may stand with their scripts in their hands. They may wish to walk around the staging area while saying their lines.

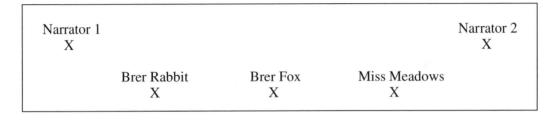

```
Narrator 1                                          Narrator 2
    X                                                   X

         Brer Rabbit        Brer Fox       Miss Meadows
              X                 X                X
```

NARRATOR 1: Now, this story here was one that came from across the big ocean—from Africa if truth be told. It came with the slaves and was told around many a campfire and many a family gathering in those days. It's the story of Brer Rabbit—surely one of the smartest and cleverest animals there ever was. Why, Brer Rabbit could fool a chicken out of her feathers and a bear out of his skin. Yep, Brer Rabbit was one of the most cunning of all animals and was a trickster through and through. Why, he just got himself into so many deeds and so many stories. Some time ago those stories was collected by Mr. Joel Chandler Harris into the Uncle Remus tales. This here story is just one of those that folks used to tell way back in the old days.

NARRATOR 2: You see, once upon a long time ago, Brer Rabbit and Brer Fox used to play all kinds of tricks on each other. They would try to fool each other to see who was the smartest, who was the cleverest.

NARRATOR 1: Now, this one day Brer Rabbit was over at Miss Meadows's house just sipping tea and watching butterflies dance through the trees.

MISS MEADOWS: So, what are you up to these days, my friend?

BRER RABBIT: Well, I've been thinking about doing some riding. It's been a long time since I've done any riding, and I just thought that it might be good to ride through the countryside.

MISS MEADOWS: But you don't have a horse, Brer Rabbit!

BRER RABBIT: Yes, I know. But you see, my old friend Brer Fox is as good as a horse. In fact, he was trained as a horse many years ago by my father, and we used to ride him through the countryside on many a fine day.

MISS MEADOWS: Well, I'll be. I didn't know that Brer Fox had been trained to be a horse.

BRER RABBIT: It's true. He's been trained by the best, and he knows how to hold a saddle and how to keep a bit in his mouth and prance around the country just like a real horse would do.

NARRATOR 2: Soon after, Brer Rabbit finished his tea and set off for home. However, when Brer Fox heard what Brer Rabbit had said about him, he stomped over to Miss Meadows's house and said in his angriest of voices:

BRER FOX: [very angrily] That Brer Rabbit sure is a liar! He's been telling stories about me that just aren't true. He better eat his words, because when I get hold of him, he's certainly going to be sorry for all that he's said.

NARRATOR 1: And with that Brer Fox stormed away and down the road. He was still angry by the time he got to Brer Rabbit's house. But by the time he got to Brer Rabbit's house he also had a plan—a plan that would quiet Brer Rabbit once and for all.

BRER FOX: Brer Rabbit, Brer Rabbit, come on out. I've come to tell you that Miss Meadows has decided to have a party and everyone is coming. I told her that I would come to fetch you, because it wouldn't be a party unless you were there.

NARRATOR 1: Now, Brer Rabbit knew that Brer Fox was a trickster and would try to trick him every chance he got. So he decided to get one up on old Brer Fox and do a little pretending to see what was on his mind.

BRER RABBIT: Is that you, Brer Fox? I can't come out now. I'm feeling sick and I shouldn't go to the party.

BRER FOX: Come out, come out! The party will be grand and it won't be the same if you're not there. Come out.

BRER RABBIT: No, I'm too sick to go to a party. It's too far to walk, and I would never make it.

BRER FOX: What if I was to carry you there?

BRER RABBIT: I'm afraid that you might drop me, and then I would be sicker than I am now.

BRER FOX: I could carry you on my back, and then you would be safe.

BRER RABBIT: But I can't ride without a saddle.

BRER FOX: Fine. I will get a saddle and put it on my back, and then you can ride to Miss Meadows's party.

BRER RABBIT: But what good is a saddle without a bridle? I will need a bridle if I am to travel safely to Miss Meadows's party.

BRER FOX: Fine. I will get a saddle and a bridle and then you can safely travel to Miss Meadows's. I will carry you most of the way to Miss Meadows's, but when we get close you will have to get down and walk the rest of the way.

BRER RABBIT: That will be fine, my friend.

NARRATOR 2: A little while later Brer Fox came back with a saddle on his back and a bridle in his mouth.

NARRATOR 1: Brer Rabbit slowly climbed on the back of Brer Fox, and the two of them set out for Miss Meadows's.

NARRATOR 2: What Brer Fox didn't know was that Brer Rabbit had secretly put on a pair of spurs. Brer Rabbit knew that his friend Brer Fox wanted to play a trick on him, so he decided to trick his friend first.

NARRATOR 1: The two friends trotted along down the road. Soon they were around the corner from Miss Meadows's house. Brer Fox had a plan to jump up and throw his friend on the ground. Everyone at Miss Meadows's party would see Brer Rabbit on the ground and they would all laugh and laugh and laugh.

NARRATOR 2: But Brer Rabbit was way ahead of Brer Fox. For he had another plan in mind.

BRER RABBIT: How are you, my friend?

BRER FOX: I am fine. Just a little tired, but I am fine.

BRER RABBIT: I have a plan. I have a plan that everyone at Miss Meadows will enjoy.

BRER FOX: What is your plan, my friend?

NARRATOR 1: With that Brer Rabbit dug his spurs into Brer Fox's sides.

NARRATOR 2: Like a shot from a rifle, Brer Fox lunged ahead. Brer Rabbit rode Brer Fox like a horse right into the middle of Miss Meadows's party. Brer Rabbit tipped his hat to Miss Meadows as he rode into the garden.

BRER RABBIT: Didn't I tell you Miss Meadows, that Brer Fox makes a fine horse? Yes, he makes a fine horse indeed.

MISS MEADOWS: You are right, Brer Rabbit, that is indeed a fine horse you have there. A mighty fine horse!

NARRATOR 1: And everyone laughed and laughed at the mighty fine horse that Brer Rabbit rode to Miss Meadows's party.

NARRATOR 2: For days afterward, everyone talked and talked about the mighty fine horse that Brer Rabbit rode to the party. A mighty fine horse indeed.

BRER FOX: [angrily] Just wait until I get my hands on Mr. Brer Rabbit. Just wait! Just wait!

Mike Fink

STAGING: Each of the characters should be standing at a lectern or a music stand. The two narrators should be placed on either side of the staging area.

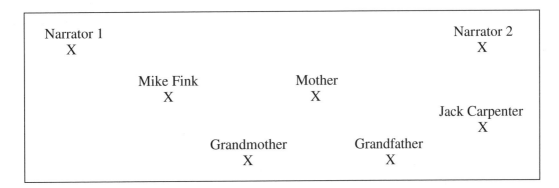

NARRATOR 1: Now it was said that in the days when America was a young country, there was a breed of men unlike any other. These were the keelboat men—some of the roughest and toughest men there were. You see, in those days cargo was carried down the Mississippi River on large barges. Goin' down to New Orleans and other cities on the river was easy—they just flowed with the current. However, after they let off their loads they had to get the keelboats back up the river. And that's where the strength of the keelboat men was needed. That's because they had to pole their heavy boats against the river. Big muscled arms and bigger than life imaginations were the hallmark of these rough and tough individuals. Nobody was stronger and nobody was meaner than a keelboat man. And of course the meanest and strongest of all the keelboat men was Mike Fink.

NARRATOR 2: Now Mike was an ornery kid even from the moment he was born. He got so tired of being cooped up indoors that he ran away from home when he was just two days old. Seems his grandfather had to go and fetch him before he got too far away.

GRANDFATHER:	What in thundernation are you doing?
MIKE FINK:	I'm just learnin' about the world.
GRANDFATHER:	Well, now, you just listen here. I want you behavin' like a normal infant. That means no more running away. You're to stay inside.
NARRATOR 1:	Well, as you might expect, Mike didn't like staying indoors. Soon as he got back to his room he jumped on the bed. That bed threw him up into the air so high that he sprang right through the roof. He came back down on the bed and bounced up into the air again—this time so high that he could see all the rivers in the west. He saw all the keelboat men polin' their keelboats up those rivers and he heard all those keelboat men singin' their songs.
NARRATOR 2:	Well, that just about did it for Mike. Soon as he bounced back down into his house, he let folks know what he wanted to do with his life.
MIKE FINK:	I aim to be a keelboat man!
GRANDMOTHER:	A what?
MIKE FINK:	A keelboat man!
GRANDMOTHER:	You can't be a keelboat man. That's no respectable job for a boy to do. That's a job for ruffians and other bad types. You just can't be a keelboat man.
MIKE FINK:	Well, that's what I'm going to be, and that's what I'm going to do!
MOTHER:	But son, are you sure that's the best kind of work for you?
MIKE FINK:	I'm sure. I'm as sure as I can be. I want to be a keelboat man.
MOTHER:	All right. It seems as though you have your heart set on being a keelboat man.
NARRATOR 1:	And with that Mike's mother put him on a wagon train headed out west.

76

NARRATOR 2: While he was out west, Mike learned how to wrestle. He learned how to shoot a rifle. And he learned how to take care of himself on the river. He became as strong as an ox and as skilled as any 10 men on the frontier.

NARRATOR 1: Well, it seems that one day he found himself face to face with Jack Carpenter, who was the King of the Keelboat men.

MIKE FINK: Howdy, friend. I'm looking for a job on the river. I'm looking to be a keelboat man.

JACK CARPENTER: [in an angry and mean voice] Ha! You think a little pipsqueak like you can be a keelboat man? Why, this river'll chew you up and spit you up faster than a mountain lion eats chickens.

MIKE FINK: I ain't afraid of no river. And I ain't afraid of no man!

JACK CARPENTER: [angrily] Are you saying that you're not afraid of the meanest and toughest and strongest keelboat man there ever was? Are you saying that you're not afraid of me?

MIKE FINK: Yup, that's what I'm saying.

JACK CARPENTER: [angrily] Well, why don't you come back when you're about 10 feet taller and when you got some muscles in your arms and some brains in your head?

MIKE FINK: I may look like I'm not much, but I'm pretty strong. Maybe I can prove it to you.

JACK CARPENTER: [forcefully] 'Bout the only thing you can prove is just how stupid you are. You see, I'm stronger than three herds of buffalo and tougher than a pack of rattlesnakes baking in the noonday sun. If you think you're tough, you're goin' to have to fight me and beat me, and there ain't no man anywhere around who can do that.

MIKE FINK: Well, let's see.

NARRATOR 2: And with that Mike and Jack began to fight. Jack charged into Mike, picked him up, and threw him clean over the Rocky Mountains.

MIKE FINK: Well, that surprised me a little. I wasn't expecting that. Looks like I'm going to need a little more practice.

NARRATOR 1: And so Mike began to practice. He started out wrestling grizzly bears. First he would wrestle with one. Then he would wrestle with two. After a while he got so good that he could wrestle a whole pack of grizzly bears with both hands tied behind his back. By then, he knew that he was ready to wrestle Jack Carpenter one more time.

NARRATOR 2: So he ran back across the Great Plains and found Jack keeling his boat up the Mississippi River.

MIKE FINK: Reckon I'm ready now for a little rematch . . . that is, if you think you can take me.

JACK CARPENTER: [angrily] You little pipsqueak, of course I can take you. I can take you jus' like a mountain lion can take a rabbit. Let's get started.

NARRATOR 1: Well, Mike and Jack began to wrestle. They wrestled up one side of the Mississippi River and down the other. They wrestled up one side of the Missouri River and down the other. They wrestled up one side of the Ohio River and down the other.

NARRATOR 2: Finally, after a few weeks of wrestling up and down all the rivers of the Midwest, Mike got Jack into a Rocky Mountain bear hug. He held on as tight as he could and finally Jack admitted defeat.

JACK CARPENTER: I guess I'm beat. You sure are one tough man. I ain't never wrestled a man as long as you and me wrestled. I guess you're ready to become a keelboat man.

NARRATOR 1: Jack taught Mike all the secrets of the river. He learned quickly and soon became one of the most well-known keelboat men of all time.

NARRATOR 2: Not only was Mike Fink one of the most respected keelboat men of all time, he was also one of the strongest. In fact, there's a story about Mike Fink and the time he wrestled a 30-foot alligator down in Louisiana. They wrestled up one side of the river and down the other. But of course you already know how that story ends.

"That's Once!"

STAGING: The two narrators should be on either side of the staging area. The other three characters should be standing at music stands or lecterns. You may wish to consider placing a cardboard cutout of a horse on the stage immediately in front of Pete Wilson and Miss Isabelle.

```
Narrator 1                                              Narrator 2
X                                                       X

        Pete Wilson      Miss Isabelle      Storekeeper
        X                X                  X
```

NARRATOR 1: Now, this here story's been told around these parts for some time now. It ain't an old story, but it's a story that people love to tell. I reckon that it has some truth in it. Don't know for sure. But you all just might want to listen to this one. Could be a lesson in here somewhere. Don't know for sure.

NARRATOR 2: Seems a while back there was this woman—Miss Isabelle was her name. Nobody could ever get along with her. She would argue. She would holler. She would make a fuss jus' about anything at all. Shoot, she was just as ornery as they come. Everybody jus' moved out of her way when she came into town to shop or to visit with the other women folk. Shoot, she just had one sharp tongue—ain't nobody could stand the way that woman talked.

NARRATOR 1: Well, this one day, believe it was about in the spring sometime, this man comes into town. He was some new feller from a town far away. Seems he had built himself a house over by the creek down by Dawson's Mill and he just was makin' his acquaintance with some of the townsfolk and loading himself up with supplies and tools and such. Getting' ready for the plantin' season, I reckon.

PETE WILSON: Howdy, I be Pete Wilson. New man in these parts, I reckon'. I just aim to settle down a bit, raise me some crops, and visit this here town of yours. Seems like a right fine place. I'm just hoping to stay a long while.

STOREKEEPER: That sounds right fine with us. We're good folks here in the valley. Mind our business and take care of our own. Where'd you say you were from, Mr. Wilson?

PETE WILSON: Well, I'm just from the other side of the state. Just wanted me some good land and a town with some good folks in it, too. This just seemed like the right place, so I just put some money down on that piece of property down by the mill and thought I'd stay a spell.

STOREKEEPER: That be fine with us, mister. I think you'll like us around here.

NARRATOR 2: Now, what Mr. Wilson didn't say was that he was also lookin' for a wife . . . someone to settle down with on his new land. He'd heard the stories about Miss Isabelle, but he didn't pay much mind to them. He just wanted himself a woman to be his wife, and he figured that Miss Isabelle would do just about right for a wife. Her sharp tongue didn't seem to bother him none.

NARRATOR 1: So he went lookin' for Miss Isabelle. Spent some time with her and finally went ahead and asked her to marry him. She thought about it for a while and figured that she wasn't going to get too many offers, not with her sharp tongue and all that, so she went right ahead and agreed to marry Pete Wilson.

NARRATOR 2: Well, they was married by the Justice of the Peace down at the County Courthouse and afterward they commenced to set out for Mr. Wilson's place. Now, I reckon before we go any further, that we should tell you 'bout that old horse of Mr. Wilson's.

NARRATOR 1: Yup, reckon we better. See, Pete's old horse was about as lame as they come. He was so old and so worn out it was a wonder that he was even walking, much less living. He was just a bundle of skin and bones and couldn't ever run even if there was a carrot waitin' for him jus' about two feet away.

NARRATOR 2: So Pete and Miss Isabelle tied on some supplies they'd picked up at the store. They put on some pots and pans, a couple of blankets, some grub, and a trunk of things from Miss Isabelle's place. Pete, he hoisted Miss Isabelle up on the horse and he climbed up on behind her. They then commenced to set off down the road for Pete's house.

NARRATOR 1: Well, that old horse must have been loaded down with too much stuff, or he was just too old and lame to carry much. He hadn't gotten but six paces down the road when he stumbled and threw old Pete, Miss Isabelle, and all their stuff into a ditch.

NARRATOR 2: They wasn't hurt or anything, and they was able to get all their stuff back up on that horse. Miss Isabelle, she never said much. But old Pete he went right around to the front of the horse and looked him straight in the eye and wagged his finger at him.

PETE WILSON: [forcefully] That's once!

NARRATOR 2: Well, they both got back on that old horse and went off down the road. They'd been goin' 'bout a mile or so when that old horse just up and stumbled once again, and they both landed right on the ground as hard as could be. 'Course, all their stuff was all over the place, too.

NARRATOR 1: Well, old Pete and Miss Isabelle both brushed themselves off, loaded up that horse again, and climbed back on. Seems as though Miss Isabelle didn't say much. I guess she was just too dazed by all the happenings. But she just held her tongue. Meanwhile, old Pete, he once again went 'round to the front of the horse, held his finger in front of the horse, and said . . .

PETE WILSON: [forcefully] That's twice!

NARRATOR 2: Well, now they was just going back down the road to old Pete's house, and wouldn't you know it, that old horse just tripped up something awful. Turned Miss Isabelle upside down and threw old Pete right into a patch of brambles. All their stuff was just scattered all over the ground.

NARRATOR 1: Well, old Pete had had it by then. He was just mad as a wet hen. He just jerked on that horse's bridle until that horse was back up on his feet. He went right around to the front of that horse, wagged his finger in that horse's face, and said . . .

PETE WILSON: [very angrily] Confound it all, that's three times!

NARRATOR 2: And with that old Pete pulled out his pistol, pointed it right between the eyes of that old horse, and—BLAM—he just shot him dead right there in the road. That old horse just fell right over—stiffer than a board—and deader than a doornail.

NARRATOR 1: Well, Miss Isabelle was so surprised that she just stood there with her mouth wide open. Finally, after she went and caught her breath, she started in on old Pete.

MISS ISABELLE: [loudly, argumentatively, and angrily] What in thunder did you do that for? Are you crazy? What did you go and do some fool thing like that? Now we ain't got no horse to carry our goods down to the house. You just went and killed the only horse we ever had. What kind of fool are you, anyway? Now we got to walk and carry all this stuff ourselves. How do you expect me to do that? I'm a right and proper lady, and I ain't going to be carryin' no stuff all the way down to your house. You must be one absolute fool to go and kill that horse the way you did. If you think I'm going to pack that stuff up on my back and carry it down this here road, then you have another think comin' We coulda walked alongside that horse while he carried all this heavy stuff. But no, you had to go and just kill him right here and now. What a fool thing to do. I just can't believe that someone would be so stupid as to shoot and kill his only horse and then make his new bride go and carry all the pots and pans herself to their new home. Why'd you go shoot him and all that? You ain't got no sense at all. Why, you must be the stupidest person I ever met. Where'd you say you was from? You come from a place of stupid people. If so, you must be one of the stupidest there ever was. Stupid, stupid, stupid! That's what you are. I just can't believe that someone with any brains at all would go and do some stupid fool act as to shoot his only horse.

NARRATOR 2: Well, Miss Isabelle went on and on and on and on. Her tongue was rattlin' worse than any snake. She was insultin' old Pete up one side and down the other. Didn't seem like she was ever goin' to stop. Old Pete just stood there staring at her. Finally, she had to stop to take a breath. Old Pete just walked right up to her, looked her right straight in the eye, and said . . .

PETE WILSON: [loudly] That's once!

The Widow and the Robbers

STAGING: The three main characters should all be seated on tall stools or chairs. They may each have a copy of the script placed on a music stand or lectern. The narrator should be standing at a podium or lectern off to the side of the staging area.

Widow X	Robber 1 X	Robber 2 X
Narrator X		

NARRATOR: Now, shortly after the Civil War there were lots of bad people on the road. People who would rob you just as soon as they would eat a meal. So it paid to be real careful. Now, one time there was this widow who had lost her husband in the Civil War. Her husband had fought for the Confederate side, and she took it real hard when she learned the news about his death. She tried to do the best she could, but raising three young un's and taking care of a house was just a lot of work for one woman to handle by herself. And to make things worse, her house was about to be taken by a Yankee money lender. Seems a few years back her husband had borrowed some money to buy the house. And now that times were bad all over the country that money lender, who just happened to be a Yankee, wanted to collect on that debt. The woman didn't know how she was ever going to pay off that debt, and she was quite worried about it. Well, late one afternoon, two men came riding up to the house.

ROBBER 1: Afternoon, ma'am. We have been riding the trail for a long time and we were wondering if we might rest a spell and get something to eat.

NARRATOR: The woman looked and noticed that both the men had Confederate jackets on. So she figured they were good men because they had fought for the same side as her husband had.

WIDOW: I reckon it would be all right. I don't have much to feed you with three children and all that, but you'd be welcome to sit at our table and take what you can.

ROBBER 2: That would be right neighborly. Thank you very kindly, ma'am.

NARRATOR: So the widow cooked them all a big meal of chicken and dumplings, green beans from the garden, and some homemade peach pie. After dinner they all went out to the front porch and sat down under a blanket of stars.

ROBBER 1: That was a mighty fine meal, ma'am. We thank you very much.

ROBBER 2: Yes, one of the finest meals I've had in quite a long time.

WIDOW: You're both welcome. I reckon I don't get many strangers here, especially Confederate strangers. It's just me and my three children and this house that we're about to lose.

ROBBER 1: What do you mean?

WIDOW: Well, you see, my late husband had to borrow some money from a Yankee trader in order for us to be able to get this place. Now that the war is over, that Yankee trader wants to get all his money back. And it seems as though I owe him $400.

ROBBER 2: I reckon he has a paper with your husband's signature on it.

WIDOW: That he does. And he's coming here tomorrow to collect that money. I just don't have that kind of money, and I'm just not sure where or when I'll ever get that kind of money. That's a lot of money for a poor widow like myself to have. I reckon I'm just going to lose my farm. I just don't know what we'll do after that. I just don't know what we'll do.

NARRATOR: The two men didn't have much to say to her. They just nodded their heads. Pretty soon after that they all went to bed. The next morning both the men came down for breakfast. There were corn cakes, fried bacon, and hot coffee for both of them.

ROBBER 1: Ma'am, me and my partner were discussin' your situation last night. And we decided that we're going to lend you that $400 so that you can pay off the mortgage.

ROBBER 2: Yup, it just seemed like the only right thing to do after all you done for us.

NARRATOR: So the two men gave the widow a bag of gold coins inside a leather pouch. Then they both got on their horses and rode off down the road. Pretty near sundown the money lender came to the door of the widow's house to see about the mortgage. He was quite surprised when the woman pulled out the leather pouch and dumped out all the gold coins on the table. However, he marked the mortgage paper "Paid in Full," signed it, and gave it over to the widow. He got back on his horse and rode back into town.

It was a little later in the evening when the woman heard someone at the door. She went downstairs and opened it up. There were the two robbers standing outside.

ROBBER 1: Good evening, ma'am.

ROBBER 2: Good evening.

WIDOW: You two boys come right in now. Let me fix you some coffee.

ROBBER 1: Thank you, ma'am.

WIDOW: Well, that mean old money lendin' Yankee came by today to take all his money. He signed the note "Paid in Full" so I guess I can keep the house now, thanks to you two boys. I aim to pay you two back any way I can. It was right nice of you to lend me that money—you didn't have to do that—but I aim to pay you back for all your kindness. I'm not sure how I'll do it, but I'll do it. My late husband would have wanted it that way.

ROBBER 2: Now, don't you worry, ma'am. You don't owe us one cent. You don't owe us anything at all.

ROBBER 1: You see, ma'am, we done waited for that money lender on the road after he left your house. And we done made his load a little lighter by collecting a tidy sum of $400 from him. I guess he just didn't know what was happening to him.

ROBBER 2: But I'll tell you one thing. He sure rode back into town faster than a bolt of greased lightning. Never saw a man so scared in all my life.

NARRATOR: It was then that the widow noticed that each of the two men was wearing a big six-shooter at his side. It was then that she knew that they were professional robbers.

ROBBER 1: So this is the way it's going to be, ma'am. We're going to leave this here leather bag full of gold coins on your table here. Seems like it's just like that leather bag we took from the lender man.

ROBBER 2: Yup. And we're just going to leave it here and be on our way. You see, your husband was a Confederate soldier, and we don't take anything from Confederate soldiers or their widows.

NARRATOR: With that the two men walked out of the house and climbed up on their horses. The widow followed them to ask their names so that she could keep them in her prayers.

ROBBER 1: That would be very nice of you, ma'am. It seems as though the two of us are in need of lots of prayers. We thank you very much.

WIDOW: But what's your names?

ROBBER 2: Well, my name is Frank James, and this here is my brother Jesse.

CHAPTER 6

Magic and Myth

Much of the folklore of America—particularly early America—is steeped in both fact and fiction. Europeans were coming to these unknown shores to discover new lands, new peoples, and new riches. Much of what they would encounter (or thought they would encounter) was unknown to them. On the other hand, indigenous people, who had lived across the continent for many centuries, had created stories and tales that explained elements of nature or celebrated the wisdom of their elders.

What resulted was a unique array of stories and tales that crossed lines, transcended boundaries, and expanded the national geography. Eventually, with each retelling, a little more imagination and a little more magic wove their way into these tales, offering reasons and explanations—but more important, celebrating the unknown parts of the world in which early peoples lived. As a result, these stories (and their counterparts) are cultural signposts that offer glimpses into the creative spirit of a people—no matter where or when they lived.

THE FOUNTAIN OF YOUTH

Many cultures and people around the world have legends about a source of eternal youth. The proverbial Fountain of Youth has always figured prominently in the tales and adventures of the explorers who came to the shores of the Americas. For reasons that are lost in time, the mythical waters of this fountain have been associated with Ponce De León and his journeys throughout this new land. It may be because he was a somewhat older explorer (in comparison to his contemporaries) or because many of his journeys took place in Florida and other southern regions where there would be a greater likelihood of finding a fountain. We will never know.

SUN AND MOON IN A BOX

In the tradition of the Zunis of the American Southwest, day and night are represented by the sun and the moon. They are also associated with summer and winter. Coyote, who is always portrayed as a cunning or meddlesome creature, disrupts the seasonal cycle by interfering with the heavenly progression. As a result everyone's life is irreversibly altered. This is one of the reasons coyote is reviled and despised and is the centerpiece of (or explanation for) many of the bad things that happen in the world.

THE SHARK CHIEF AND THE GREAT WAVE

In this classic tale of long ago, native Hawaiians forget to take care of the earth and sea. As a result, they must pay the (environmental) consequences. In this version I decided to alter the time frame of the original story slightly so that all the events would take place in a 24-hour period. As in the traditional version, I focused on the power and might of a single tsunami wave rather than a series of waves (a wave train of three to ten waves) typical of most tsunamis. Finally, the script concludes with hope and an environmental promise for the ancient Hawaiians as well as modern-day readers.

THE FLEA

This story has strong Mexican roots and is typical of folktales that are part of the fabric of everyday life in the Hispanic Southwest. This particular tale originated on the southern edge of the San Luis Valley (Colorado) near the New Mexico border. It is a variant of a common story with an international theme. In many of the variations, the hero hides from the devil; in other retellings there is a battle between the forces of good and evil.

GRANDMOTHER SPIDER STEALS THE SUN

This story teaches children (and adults) to respect nature and all its creatures—both large and small. It originated with the Cherokee people, who, like Grandmother Spider, make clay bowls. Just like Grandmother Spider, the Cherokee place their bowls of soft clay in a cool, dark place to harden. Then the Cherokee people put their bowls in a hot fire to strengthen them. By the same token, Grandmother Spider hardened her bowl by carrying the sun inside it. The story is both a celebration of one specific creature and a paean to her remarkable journey.

The Fountain of Youth

STAGING: The three narrators should be standing in a row along the back of the staging area. Each should be standing in front of a music stand holding a script. The character of Ponce De León should be seated on a chair in the front of the staging area. If possible, drape a robe (or large beach towel) over the shoulders of Ponce De León. This character should speak in a slow and "royal" manner.

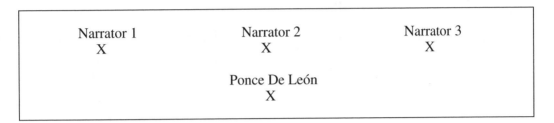

NARRATOR 1: In the Spanish court of the late fifteenth and early sixteenth centuries, there was a handsome man of great bearing—Juan Ponce De León. He was rumored to have been very successful with many ladies and, indeed, they were all quite taken with him.

NARRATOR 2: Ponce De León made many voyages of discovery to new places and new lands. He even sailed on the second voyage of Columbus to the New World.

NARRATOR 3: He brought back many riches for his home country of Spain. There was plenty of gold for the treasury. There were also new lands to control throughout the New World.

PONCE DE LEÓN: [slowly, but with dignity] Ah, those were truly good years. We sailed across the wide ocean and found lands that no one had ever seen before—at least no white man had ever seen. My men and I sailed to Puerto Rico, where we set up mines and plantations. We took many riches from the soil—minerals and crops alike. We were able to extend the Spanish empire in many places—adding to our domain of both land and sea. We were a powerful force—a force to be reckoned with—and a force that was more powerful than any put forth by another country. It was a good time for exploration and a good time to make many new discoveries. There were riches to be found everywhere we looked.

NARRATOR 1: Ponce De León was rewarded for all his discoveries and all he brought back to Spain with much fame and much fortune. The king gave him many grants to equip his expeditions and to colonize new islands in the name of Spain.

NARRATOR 2: Ah, but there were also some penalties to be paid as well. The hot winds that constantly blew across the sea had roughened the face of Ponce De León. The youth that had once been his trademark had all but been erased from his person. He was no longer the dashing young hero who had swayed the ladies of the court.

NARRATOR 3: He had been in many battles and many conflicts. His bones were tired and weary from all the fighting. He had suffered wounds, and some had not healed properly due to improper medical care. His body ached and his body hurt, and he walked slowly from place to place. His strength was not what it had been many years ago. Age was slowly creeping up on him. He was no longer the strong warrior.

PONCE DE LEÓN: [slowly, but with strength] I wish I had the body of my youth. I wish I had the strength and stamina of my younger days. But the battles we have fought and the seas we have sailed have all taken their toll on me. I ache in places I never ached before. I hurt in places that should not hurt. My pace is much slower now. My voice is not as strong as it once was because I have spent much time shouting orders to my men and commanding large groups of people in service to my king. I do not wish to admit this, but I am a weaker man. My strength is ebbing, and I feel the pains of old age creeping into my everyday life. Oh, how I wish there was a way for me to regain the

94

strength and vigor of my youth. Then I would be that great and powerful leader again. Then we would be able to continue our voyages and continue our discoveries to new lands and, of course, new riches.

NARRATOR 1: It was then that Ponce De León heard a most powerful rumor. A local woman from the hills above the garrison where Ponce De León and his men were stationed told the story of an enchanted island where some of her people had gone. She told of how those people had gone to the island in search of fruits and other foods to bring back to the village. What they brought back was even more nourishing than bunches of bananas or baskets of mangoes.

NARRATOR 2: It was told that there was a magical spring on this island. The woman told of a spring that gushed water with magical powers—the power to restore youth, the power to magically erase all signs of old age. She told of how her kinsmen had traveled to this island and had stayed for a long time—perhaps many years. Yet when these people returned, they had not aged a single day. They all had the faces of young people, they all had the skin of their youth. It was as though they had grown younger while they were away, younger rather than older.

NARRATOR 3: Ponce De León listened to the story and his eyes filled with hope. Here, he thought, I will regain my youth. Here, he thought, I will regain the power and strength that was once mine. Here, he began to believe, I will assume the power of my early days—a power that made him one of the most courageous and strongest explorers to ever sail the oceans of the world.

PONCE DE LEÓN: [in a powerful voice] The Fountain of Youth shall be mine, and I will consume its waters and become a new man again. Come, let us sail! Come, let us strike out and find this Fountain! Come, let us seek its eternal strength! Sail on!

NARRATOR 1: Ponce De León gathered his men together, and they set out on a northward voyage. They sailed for many days and eventually sighted land. As they approached they saw a wide river and a long sandy beach that sloped down from a rich tropical forest.

NARRATOR 2: Ponce De León landed at the mouth of the river and claimed this new land for Spain. The first mate noted that the landing occurred at the time of the Easter feast—also known as *Pascua Florida* in Spanish. As a result, the land was named La Florida. It is now known as the state of Florida.

NARRATOR 3: Ponce De León and his men began to explore this new land. They traveled to far places in constant search for the Fountain of Youth. Failing to find it, they sailed around the tip of La Florida and explored the land along the Gulf Coast. Alas, all their searching was in vain, for they never did find the Fountain as it was described to them by the woman of the village.

PONCE DE LEÓN: [dejected and somewhat weaker] Alas, we could not locate the mystical Fountain of Youth. My men and I have searched in many places, but there is no Fountain to be found. Perhaps the Fountain was only a story made up by the people of this land. Perhaps the Fountain never really existed. Perhaps we are to be thought fools for ever believing that there was something as simple as a Fountain of Youth—a fountain that would return us to the days of our youth. I do not know. Perhaps I will never know. But we have accomplished one thing. We have discovered many new lands. We have discovered many new places. And Spain will be all the richer for our discoveries. Perhaps that will be our legacy. Perhaps that will be what we are remembered for the most.

NARRATOR 1: Ponce De León and his men continued to search for the mythical Fountain of Youth throughout the Caribbean islands. But they never did find the fulfillment of their dreams.

NARRATOR 2: Years later, Ponce De León returned to Florida in order to properly claim it for Spain. While in a battle with some of the native Indians, he was severely wounded. He was taken to Cuba to heal from his wounds.

NARRATOR 3: Alas, he tragically died while he was in Cuba. Alas, he was never able to find the immortal Fountain of Youth. Alas, he died an old man—an old man who sought forever youth, yet who discovered the richness of a new world. Youth would not be his, but there was an even greater treasure to be claimed in the land of this new world. However, the fates of time and the legacy of history would remember Ponce De León, not for the new lands he found, but rather for what he never found . . . for what he never discovered . . . for what would never be his.

Sun and Moon in a Box

STAGING: The narrator should be standing behind a lectern or podium. The two main characters (Eagle, Coyote) should be walking about the staging area as they speak their lines. They may wish to hold a small cardboard box during the presentation.

Narrator X			
	Coyote X	[box]	Eagle X

NARRATOR: Once upon a time—in a time long before there was a sun or a moon—Eagle and Coyote were hunting in the desert. After flying over a canyon and swimming across a river, they came to Kachina Pueblo. The Kachinas were dancing, so Eagle and Coyote watched them. They noticed that near the dance there was a large square box.

COYOTE: That looks like a fine box.

EAGLE: That must be where the sun and the moon are kept. I have heard many good things about the sun and the moon.

COYOTE: Perhaps we should steal the box.

EAGLE: That would be wrong. Why don't we just borrow it?

NARRATOR: And so that is what they did. Eagle grabbed the box and flew off. Coyote ran after him along the ground. After a while Coyote called to Eagle.

COYOTE: Hey, my friend let me have the box. I am ashamed to let you do all the carrying.

EAGLE: No, you are not reliable. You might open the box and we would lose the wonderful things we borrowed.

NARRATOR: They continued their journey—Eagle flew over the ground and Coyote ran along underneath the great bird. Once more, Coyote called to his friend.

COYOTE: I am ashamed to let you carry the box. If I don't help you, people will talk badly about me. Let me help you.

EAGLE: No, I don't trust you. Curiosity will get the better of you and you will open the box.

COYOTE: Do not fear, my friend. I would not do such a thing. But if I don't help in some way, people will say that I am lazy and disrespectful.

EAGLE: No, I won't give this box to you.

NARRATOR: The two animals continued on as before. Eagle was flying and Coyote was running. One more time, Coyote begged to carry the box.

COYOTE: Let me carry the box for a while. My children will not respect me if they learn that I did not help my friend with his load.

EAGLE: Will you promise not to drop the box? Will you promise not to open the box if I let you carry it?

COYOTE: I promise. I promise! You can trust me. I will not betray your trust.

NARRATOR: So Eagle flew down and gave the box to Coyote. They continued on as before. Eagle was flying and Coyote was running with the box in his mouth. Soon they came to a large wooded area with lots of trees and bushes.

COYOTE: I am very curious about this box. I think I will hide from my friend in the middle of all these bushes.

EAGLE: Where is my friend, Coyote? I wonder if he has become curious about the contents of the box. I hope he doesn't open the box.

COYOTE: This is a special box. I wonder what is inside. I think I will open it up.

NARRATOR: In a flash, Sun came out of the box and flew to the very edge of the sky.

COYOTE: I must get the lid back on the box as quickly as I can, or something else will surely happen.

NARRATOR: But before Coyote could put the lid back on the box, Moon jumped out and soared to the outer rim of the sky. With both the Sun and Moon in the sky, the world grew cold. Leaves fell from the trees, the grass turned brown, and snow fell across the land.

EAGLE: I should have known better than to give anything to Coyote. He just cannot be trusted; he can never keep a promise. Now, because of him, we have winter. Sun and Moon are far away and the summer is much shorter. It is all Coyote's fault. Coyote caused the winter. He is the one to blame.

NARRATOR: And from that day forward Sun and Moon have lived in the far reaches of the sky. Winter came upon the land, and the summer was short. All because of Coyote and his curiosity.

The Shark Chief and the Great Wave

STAGING: Each of the characters should be at a lectern or podium. The narrator should be positioned to one side of the staging area, on a high stool or tall chair.

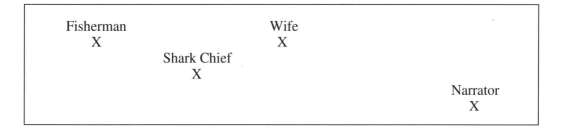

Fisherman
X

Wife
X

Shark Chief
X

Narrator
X

NARRATOR: In a long-ago time there lived in the rippling waters of the Big Island the great Shark Chief. The Shark Chief observed the Hawaiian people and his large black eyes often filled with anger.

In this time people took all their bounty from the sea and land. It was a time when women harvested fruits from the forests but never planted crops. It was a time when men plucked fish from the ocean, but always in the same place. The rich green earth and bright blue sea were forgotten as the people kept taking from their surroundings, never thinking of the consequences.

SHARK CHIEF: The people forget who provides for them. They take too much from the land and give nothing back. They do not conserve the riches of the sea. In time, there will be nothing left.

NARRATOR: In a small village that hugged the black sand beach of the Waipi'o Valley, a poor fisherman lived with his wife. Each day the fisherman went out in his hand-hewn canoe of koa wood to fish the waters. Each day his wife went out with other women to

From *American Folklore, Legends, and Tall Tales for Readers Theatre* by Anthony D. Fredericks. Westport, CT: Teacher Ideas Press. Copyright © 2008.

pick breadfruit and sweet bananas from the nearby forests.

At day's end, when dusk had fallen upon the village, the fisherman and his wife prepared their evening meal. But after a time there were fewer fish. And there was less fruit. There was little food to share.

FISHERMAN: Each day we work hard and each day there is less for us to eat.

WIFE: Soon there will be no food from the land, and the sea will be barren.

FISHERMAN: What will we do then? I do not know how we will survive.

NARRATOR: The fisherman and his wife sat in the silence of their hut and ate their meager meal as the darkness surrounded them.

The next morning a fiery sun peeked above the mountain ridge. The fisherman launched his boat earlier than usual and set out for the traditional fishing grounds. The sun's radiance splashed many colors across the water as he cast out his baited hooks. He waited patiently.

After a long time the fisherman pulled in his lines. Nothing. Only bits of seaweed were tangled around his hooks. He let the lines down once again.

The sun began to arc overhead, casting the clouds in shades of pink and white. The whole sky looked like the inside of a conch shell freshly plucked from the ocean floor. But there were no fish in that ocean—only empty hooks and tangled lines.

The sun slowly arced overhead and still the fisherman had nothing to show for his labors. He was angry and shook his fist at the sea.

FISHERMAN: O, spirits of the sea, you do not care that a poor fisherman works early and labors late. You do not care that there are no fish to feed my wife and me.

102

Today, and every day, you send nothing to my hooks but bits of seaweed and empty promises. You do not care if this fisherman dies. I say you are not spirits! If indeed the sea is bountiful, then send fish to my lines. Fill my boat and let me eat.

NARRATOR: The once still waters began to churn and boil. Foaming waves rose high above the tiny canoe. Dark clouds, black as night, gathered in the sky and cast the ocean in deep shadows. The wind blew from several directions. Lightning flashed. Thunder boomed.

Then suddenly, from out of the angry sea, rose the great Shark Chief. Fear washed over the fisherman. He threw himself into the bottom of the canoe, his head buried in his hands.

FISHERMAN: Forgive my words; they were said in haste and were not my true beliefs.

NARRATOR: The Shark Chief swam slowly around the canoe. At last he reared his head above the canoe and spoke to the frightened fisherman.

SHARK CHIEF: You say there is no bounty! You say there are no fish in the waters or food upon the land! It is because the people do not care for their surroundings. They overfish the waters. They do not plant crops or tend the forests. Do you not know from where your bounty comes?

NARRATOR: The fisherman cowered in the bottom of his canoe.

FISHERMAN: O great Shark Chief, I beg you, forgive me.

NARRATOR: Again, the Shark Chief circled the tiny canoe and once more reared his head above the waves.

SHARK CHIEF: The people of Hawai'i must pay a price. I shall cause a Great Wave, a tsunami, to rise from the depths of the ocean. It shall tower to the sky and blot out the sun. The wave will be filled with rage and great fury. Nothing shall escape its wrath. It will

103

SPEED across the sea and into the land. The island will be swept clean and readied for a new beginning.

FISHERMAN: Oh Shark Chief, please spare me. I promise I will always care for the land on which I live. I promise I will never overfish the deep blue waters. I am not evil. I will honor my surroundings in the ways of my ancestors. I will not forget from where my bounty comes. I will always remember.

NARRATOR: The large black eyes of the Shark Chief gazed upon the man. He took pity on the poor fisherman.

SHARK CHIEF: I have heard your promise. For that, I will grant your wish. But I cannot do so for the other people of the village. Take your wife. Climb to the top of Mauna Kea, the tallest mountain on the island, and wait there. I will send a Great Wave across the island, cleansing it of evil and purifying it. Remain on the mountain and you will be saved.

NARRATOR: At once the Shark Chief slipped beneath the waves. The waters calmed and the wind was still. The fisherman paddled to the shore with long strokes. On reaching the beach he leaped from the boat and ran to his hut.

FISHERMAN: [to wife] We must go. The Shark Chief will cause a Great Wave, a tsunami, to sweep over the island. We must save ourselves!

WIFE: Then let us leave now. There is no time to gather our few belongings.

NARRATOR: The pair scrambled up the side of the ancient volcano. The blood-red glow of the late afternoon sun sprayed wild colors across the ground. They clambered over jagged boulders and rough lava rocks. They cut their hands and feet on the sharp grasses that grew beside the path. Their journey was difficult and tiring. They said nothing to one another as they hastened up the mountain.

Finally they arrived at the top. They looked across the land and down to the sea far below. They were saddened at what they saw, for they knew that it would soon be gone. In a grieving voice, the woman began to chant.

WIFE: O Hawai'i, my home,
You shall be forever lost!
Your bright shining beaches,
And your sweet forests of green,
Will be covered by the angry sea.
The waters will flow over the villages.
They will destroy the temples and huts.
They will extinguish the cooking fires.
And the sounds of the people will be gone.
The hula drums will be silenced.
As will the laughter of children.
No more will our people dance and sing.
Only the sea will remain.
And the sea is powerful.
It will cover Hawai'i,
And the place of our ancestors will be changed forever.

NARRATOR: The air was still and there was a silence all around. Then, from far out at sea came a booming roar. The fisherman and his wife gazed in awe as a great wall of water rose from the surface of the ocean and rushed toward the island—a tsunami! The foaming monster grew larger and larger until it blotted out the sky. Its thunder echoed through the valleys and across the mountaintop. BOOM! BOOM!

The Great Wave was filled with fury as it rushed over beaches and crashed through the valleys. It roared across the landscape, sending fists of power into the villages. Buildings crumpled, temples collapsed, and people were swept away. Nothing, except the mountain, could withstand its strength.

105

The Great Wave rose upon the land and crept up the side of Mauna Kea. It was like a growling beast—full of might, full of wrath.

The fisherman and his wife looked about and saw that they were on a tiny island of rock in the middle of a churning sea. The ocean did not rise any further. No more waves came from off the sea. But the boiling water was all around them.

FISHERMAN: The Shark Chief has unleashed his temper upon the land.

WIFE: But he has spared us, as he said he would.

NARRATOR: At last, weak and tired, the fisherman and his wife fell asleep beneath a cool blanket of stars. When they awoke the next morning the ocean had returned to its rightful place. As they looked about them they could see a barren island that had once been their home. There were no villages. There were no long green forests or palm trees heavy with sweet coconuts. The island had been swept clean by the might of the Shark Chief's wave.

With sad hearts, the fisherman and his wife walked down the face of the mountain. They found the place where once their hut had stood. But now there was only tumbled sand and broken lava rock.

The fisherman and his wife stood on the black sand beach and looked out over the sea. The Shark Chief rose from out of the rippling waters and watched them with his large black eyes.

FISHERMAN: O great Shark Chief, we shall always remember from where our bounty comes. We shall not overpick the forests. We shall replenish the earth with fields of kalo and sweet potatoes. We shall not overfish the ocean. We shall take our fish from many different waters. We shall use your gifts wisely. We shall care for the land and sea from this day forward.

106

NARRATOR: The teeth of the Shark Chief gleamed white as bone as he slid beneath the waves. As the fisherman and his wife stood on the beach, they saw something bobbing on the waves. Slowly, it floated to the shore and came to rest on the sand. It was the fisherman's canoe. They dragged it up on the beach. Flapping in the bottom were two *aku* fish.

FISHERMAN: The Shark Chief has remembered us, and we, too, shall remember our surroundings. We promise to renew the earth, take care of the ocean, and give praise every day for our bounty.

WIFE: The Shark Chief is very good.

NARRATOR: Together they danced a hula on the beach and were thankful for their safety.

In time the Big Island was bountiful with crops and the seas were rich with fish. And the people of Hawai'i remembered their promise and never forgot the Shark Chief or the Great Wave.

The Flea

STAGING: The two narrators should be positioned on either side of the staging area behind a lectern or music stand. The other three characters should be on tall stools or chairs in the middle of the staging area.

```
Narrator 1                                              Narrator 2
X                                                       X


        Pedro              Magician              Maria
        X                  X                     X
```

NARRATOR 1: In a long-ago time in the territory of Colorado in the southwest of this country there lived a man who was a great magician. This magician had great powers and was a very wise magician. There are those who would say that he was the devil himself—but they would not, of course, ever say that to his face.

NARRATOR 2: Now that great magician, that man, had a very beautiful daughter. Maria was her name, and she was, indeed, *muy bonita*—very beautiful. And, as one might expect, his daughter's hand was sought by all the young men of the village. But there was only one boy who truly captured her heart, and his name was Pedro. She loved Pedro with all her being, with all her soul.

MAGICIAN: My dear Maria. I know that you love Pedro with all your heart and with all your soul. I know that you wish to marry him in the *zócalo*—the village square.

MARIA: Yes, father, I am very much in love with Pedro. He is my heart's desire, and I wish to live my life with him.

MAGICIAN: Very well, my daughter. I will let you marry him if he can outsmart me.

NARRATOR 1: With that, Maria ran to tell Pedro of the news. She told him that they could marry if he could only outsmart her father.

NARRATOR 2: And so Pedro went to the house of Maria's father to ask for his daughter's hand in marriage.

MAGICIAN: [to Pedro] Pedro, I know that you are in love with my daughter. So if, over the next *tres noches* (three nights) you can sleep where my spells cannot find you, then I will gladly give my daughter's hand to you in holy matrimony.

NARRATOR 1: Now there is one thing that you need to know about young Pedro. You see, Pedro was also a magician. But the father did not know this. In fact, there was no one in the entire village who knew that Pedro was just as smart and just as magical as Maria's *padre* (father).

NARRATOR 2: So Pedro thought long and hard, and on the first night he rocked himself to sleep on the horns of the moon.

MAGICIAN: [to Pedro] *Buenas dias*—good morning, Pedro. How did you sleep last night? It must have been very uncomfortable sleeping on the moon.

PEDRO: How did you know that?

MAGICIAN: Remember that I am a magician and that I know everything!

NARRATOR 1: Pedro was amazed. So he began to think again. He thought long and hard.

PEDRO: Hmm. I wonder where I should sleep tonight. Where can I sleep so that the magician doesn't know where I am?

NARRATOR 2: On the second night Pedro slept deep inside *un esqueleto* (a shell) on the very bottom of the ocean. He was sure that the old magician would never know he was there.

109

MAGICIAN: Good morning again, Pedro. I would imagine that you are very fond of salt since you spent the night sleeping at the bottom of the sea.

PEDRO: You are correct. But how did you know?

MAGICIAN: A good magician should never tell his secrets, Pedro. Remember now, you have only one more night left. Will you discover a place to sleep where my spells cannot find you?

PEDRO: I think I can. In fact, I am sure of it.

[to Maria] My dear Maria, your father has given me a very difficult challenge to win your hand in marriage. But I will prevail. I will find a place where his spells cannot locate me.

MARIA: I hope so, my love. Remember that I shall be here waiting for you.

NARRATOR 1: Pedro went to the side of the door and turned himself into a flea. He hopped onto the door jamb and waited.

NARRATOR 2: Soon the magician went outside to cast his spells. As he passed by the door, the enchanted flea jumped onto the rim of his *sombrero* (hat) and hid.

MAGICIAN: Where did that boy go? Where is he? I cannot find him! I have looked up and I have looked down, but he is nowhere to be found. I just don't understand—he couldn't just have disappeared into thin air. He must be somewhere, but I can't see him anywhere. I just don't understand.

NARRATOR 1: Finally the magician gave up and decided to go back home. The flea was still perched on the rim of his hat and traveled back to the house with the magician.

NARRATOR 2: When the magician went in through the door, the flea hopped back onto the door jamb. He soon settled down for a good night's *sueño* (sleep).

NARRATOR 1: The next morning Pedro went to the magician's house to wish him a good day.

PEDRO: [to Magician] Good morning, sir. I slept very well. I wonder if you can tell me where I slept last night.

MAGICIAN: I just don't know. I don't have any idea where you slept. It seems as though you have outwitted me. And in the bargain, you have won my daughter's hand in marriage.

MARIA: [to Pedro] Oh, Pedro, Oh, Pedro!! You are so clever! You are so smart! Now at last we can marry and live our life together.

NARRATOR 2: And so it was that Pedro and Maria were soon married in a grand ceremony in the center of the *zócalo*.

NARRATOR 1: And on the first night of their marriage they slept on the horns of the moon.

NARRATOR 2: And on the second night of their marriage they slept inside a shell on the bottom of the sea.

NARRATOR 1: And on the third night of their marriage they turned themselves into fleas . . . .

NARRATOR 2: And where did they sleep?

NARRATOR 1: They slept on the rim of her father's sombrero . . . .

NARRATOR 2: And lived happily ever after—*con mucho amor*!

Grandmother Spider Steals the Sun

STAGING: The characters should all be standing behind lecterns or music stands. The narrator should be seated on a stool or high chair in the front of the staging area.

Wolf	Coyote	Possum	Buzzard	Grandmother Spider
X	X	X	X	X

Narrator
X

NARRATOR: It was a long, long time ago when half the world was in darkness. One half of the world had the sun, but the other half of the world was always cast in darkness. All the animals lived in the dark part of the world, and all the animals were always bumping into one another because they could not see through the darkness.

WOLF: This is not good. Everyone is bumping into one another. Everyone is bumping into me. I don't like it when everyone bumps into me in the darkness.

COYOTE: What do you think we should do, my friend?

WOLF: I think that we should go to the other side of the world and ask them to share a piece of the sun with us.

COYOTE: They will never share a piece of the sun with us. They want to keep the sun all for themselves.

WOLF: I think that if we ask them nicely they would share a small piece of the sun with us. Then we could have light in our part of the world. Then everybody wouldn't be bumping into each other all the time.

COYOTE: I think you are wrong, my friend. Why would they want to share a piece of the sun with us? They have had the sun for all these years and have never offered to share even a small part of it with us. I think they want it all for themselves.

WOLF: Maybe they haven't shared the sun with us because we've never asked them before.

COYOTE: I think you're wrong. I think that we should be sure that we get what is due to us. I think that we should sneak over to the other side of the world and steal a piece of the sun.

WOLF: Steal a piece of the sun!!

COYOTE: That's right. We can steal just a little piece of the sun and they will never miss it. How could they miss just a little piece of the sun when they have so much sun for themselves?

NARRATOR: And so all the animals decided that they should sneak over to the other side of the world and steal a little piece of the sun. The animals began to talk among themselves about how they would get to the other side of the world, how they would gather up a little piece of the sun, and how they would bring that small piece of the sun back to their side of the world. The discussion was very lively. The discussion was very animated. The discussion was very intense Then, there was a small voice from the back of the cave in which all the animals had gathered.

WOLF: Who goes there?

POSSUM: It is me. I can get the sun.

COYOTE: You! What makes you think that you can go to the other side of the world and steal a piece of the sun?

POSSUM: Well, you see, I have these very sharp claws. That means that I can dig a tunnel. I will dig a long tunnel to the other side of the world.

WOLF: What a great idea! A tunnel!!

POSSUM: When I get to the other side of the world I will take a little piece of the sun and hide it in my big bushy tail. Then I will run all the way back through the tunnel and bring everybody the sun.

COYOTE: That's a great idea!

NARRATOR: So Possum went to the back of the cave and began to dig a tunnel with his sharp claws. Soon the tunnel was very, very deep and was all the way to the other side of the world. Possum crawled out and the light from the sun hit his eyes.

POSSUM: My, that sun is very bright. I think I will just take a little piece of the sun.

NARRATOR: And so Possum stole a little piece of the sun and tucked it into his big bushy tail. He ran back down the tunnel—back to where he started.

POSSUM: Oh, my! What is that burning smell? Something is burning, and I don't know what it is.

NARRATOR: When Possum got back to the cave all the other animals yelled at him.

ALL ANIMALS: Possum, Possum, your tail is burning. YOUR TAIL IS BURNING!

NARRATOR: Wolf threw some water on Possum's tail and put out the fire. But when all the smoke had cleared everybody noticed that all the hair on Possum's tail had been burned by the sun. There was no more fur on his tail—none at all! And you know, Possum's tail has been that way ever since.

WOLF: We still don't have any sun. What should we do? What should we do?

BUZZARD: I'll go! I'll go!

COYOTE: What makes you think you can capture a piece of the sun for us?

BUZZARD: I can fly to the other side of the world, steal a small piece of the sun, and fly back here really fast. And I won't be silly enough to hide the piece of sun in my tail. I'm going to hide it in the beautiful crown of feathers on my head.

NARRATOR: And with that, Buzzard flew through the tunnel and out to the other side of the world. He quickly stole a little piece of the sun, tucked it into the crown of feathers on his head, and flew back down the tunnel as fast as he could. But just as he flew back into the cave where all the other animals were, they all noticed smoke coming from Buzzard's head.

ALL ANIMALS: Buzzard, Buzzard, your head is on fire. YOUR HEAD IS ON FIRE!

NARRATOR: Wolf threw some water on the top of Buzzard's head and put out the fire. But when all the smoke had cleared everybody noticed that all the feathers on Buzzard's head had been burned by the sun. There were no more feathers on his head—none at all! And you know, Buzzard's head has been that way ever since.

WOLF: Well, Possum wasn't able to get a piece of the sun for us. And Buzzard wasn't able to get a

piece of the sun for us. Who will be able to get a piece of the sun?

GRANDMOTHER SPIDER: I'll go! I'll go!

WOLF: Grandmother Spider, how can you go? You are so tiny! You are so old! You will never be able to make it to the other side of the world. It is a long way and it is very dangerous. It was dangerous for Possum. And it was dangerous for Buzzard. What makes you think that you can steal a piece of the sun when animals bigger and younger than you could not?

GRANDMOTHER SPIDER: I may be old and I may be small—but age and size have little to do with being smart. I will be able to get a piece of the sun and bring light and warmth to our part of the world. All I need is a piece of clay.

NARRATOR: Wolf went to get a piece of clay for Grandmother Spider. As all the other animals watched, Grandmother Spider sat in the middle of the room and began to fashion a small pot out of the clay. When she was done, she lifted the pot onto her back and scrambled into the tunnel. It took her a long, long time to get to the other side of the world. Finally, she crept out of the tunnel and over to the sun. She took a little piece of sun and put it into her pot. She scrambled back home. As soon as she entered the cave the piece of sun grew larger and larger and larger. Finally, it got so big that it burst out of the cave and up into the sky.

WOLF: Look, Grandmother Spider has captured the sun!

COYOTE: She did it! She did what nobody else could do. She captured the sun!

POSSUM: Now we will have the sun to give us light.

BUZZARD: Now we will have the sun to give us warmth.

ALL ANIMALS: Hooray for Grandmother Spider! HOORAY FOR GRANDMOTHER SPIDER!!

NARRATOR: From that day to the present, Grandmother Spider has always included the shape of the sun in her web. And if you look very closely at a spider's web, you will see the shape of the sun in the very center of that web. It is the very sun that Grandmother Spider—though she was small and old—was able to capture from the other side of the world. Every spider today makes sure that there is a sun in the middle of its web. That sun is in honor of Grandmother Spider, who gave us all light and warmth.

CHAPTER 7

Ballads and Songs

The songs of America are both classic and perceptive. They provide us with a unique look inside the times (both good and bad) of a diverse group of people as they settled the land, farmed its soil, praised its bounty, and endured its hardships. Music was, and always has been, a balm for the dangers of early American life and a respite in times of trouble. Long before the invention of iPods and hip-hop ring tones, people gathered around a campfire or in a local meeting house (e.g., a tavern) to entertain themselves with song. Songs were a solace as much as they were the predominant entertainment of the day.

The songs our ancestors sang and the tunes they composed were simple in scope, but they were also windows into their lives and beliefs. The collection in this chapter provides you and your students with readers theatre adaptations that open up new lines of discovery and exploration. Here students will find the heart and soul of Americans from North and South, East and West.

YANKEE DOODLE

This popular American song has its origins in the Revolutionary War. It is said that it was originally composed by a doctor in the English Army who simply wanted to embarrass the American troops—who were seen as nothing more than a ragtag bunch of misfits. However, the American troops soon adopted the song and sang it throughout the war as they won battle after battle. It has had many variations over the years—the following version is as close to the original as can be authenticated.

OLD SMOKY

This is a traditional American folk song that laments a love won . . . and then lost. It is believed that Old Smoky may be a high mountain somewhere in the Ozark Mountains or perhaps in the central Appalachian range. This song has been successfully recorded by several musical groups, and each bears the distinctive stamp of bluegrass music, a musical form that had its origins in the Irish and Scottish heritage of the people who settled this particular region of the United States.

HOME ON THE RANGE

If ever there was a classic song of the American West, this would be it! This song celebrates the life of the cowboy: wide open spaces, a solitary existence, and endless seas of wildlife as far as the eye could see. It is not only a celebration of our past, but a remembrance of the land as it was before fast-food restaurants, cheap motels, and interstate highways appeared over every horizon or around every mountain peak. It was a simpler life, to be sure, but the song is as American as they come.

BUFFALO GALS

First performed in 1844, this ditty has become one of the classic American tunes of the nineteenth century. The "Buffalo" in "Buffalo Gals" refers to the city of Buffalo, New York, rather than to the beasts that roamed the great American frontier or to the regiments of "Buffalo Soldiers" (African American troops) that were part of the U.S. Army. The song became so popular that traveling minstrels frequently changed the lyrics to suit the town in which it was sung. As a result, it might be performed as "Boston Gals" or "New York Gals" when sung in those cities.

THE COWBOY'S LAMENT

Although this ballad (also known as "The Streets of Laredo") is a classic American tune, its origins are more European than Western. It is believed that this song descended from a late eighteenth-century Irish/British folk song "The Unfortunate Rake." The original song has been modified and rewritten over the years to become a ballad in which a dying cowboy provides good advice to a living one. The song was successfully recorded by many artists and groups throughout the mid-twentieth century.

Yankee Doodle

STAGING: The chorus may consist of from three to six members, each of whom should be seated on a tall stool or chair with a music stand or lectern in front. The other characters may be scattered across the staging area in a random fashion, perhaps with a script in their hands.

```
                                    Chorus
                                  X   X   X
                                    X   X
            Reader 1
               X              Reader 2
                                 X
                                                      Reader 3
                                                         X
            Reader 4              Reader 5
               X                    X
   Reader 6
      X                                    Reader 7
                                              X
```

READER 1: Father and I went down to camp,
Along with Captain Goodwin.
And there we saw the men and boys,
As thick as hasty pudding.

CHORUS: Yankee Doodle, keep it up,
Yankee Doodle dandy!
Mind the music and the steps,
And with the girls be handy!

READER 2: There was Captain Washington,
Upon a slapping stallion,
Giving orders to his men,
I guess there was a million.

CHORUS: Yankee Doodle, keep it up,
Yankee Doodle dandy!
Mind the music and the steps,
And with the girls be handy!

READER 3: And there they had a swamping gun,
As big as a log of maple,
On a deuced little cart,
A load for father's cattle.

CHORUS: Yankee Doodle, keep it up,
Yankee Doodle dandy!
Mind the music and the steps,
And with the girls be handy!

READER 4: And every time they fired it off,
It took a horn of powder;
It made a noise like father's gun,
Only a nation louder.

CHORUS: Yankee Doodle, keep it up,
Yankee Doodle dandy!
Mind the music and the steps,
And with the girls be handy!

READER 5: And there I saw a little keg,
Its heads were made of leather.
They knocked upon it with little sticks,
To call the folks together.

CHORUS: Yankee Doodle, keep it up,
Yankee Doodle dandy!
Mind the music and the steps,
And with the girls be handy!

READER 6: The troopers, too, would gallop up,
And fire right in our faces.
It scared me almost half to death,
To see them run such races.

CHORUS: Yankee Doodle, keep it up,
Yankee Doodle dandy!
Mind the music and the steps,
And with the girls be handy!

READER 7: But I can't tell you half I saw,
They kept up such a smother,
So I took off my hat, made a bow,
And scampered home to mother.

CHORUS: Yankee Doodle, keep it up,
Yankee Doodle dandy!
Mind the music and the steps,
And with the girls be handy!

Old Smoky

STAGING: The players may be randomly placed across the staging area. Each should be seated on a tall stool or chair. They may hold their scripts in their hands or use music stands.

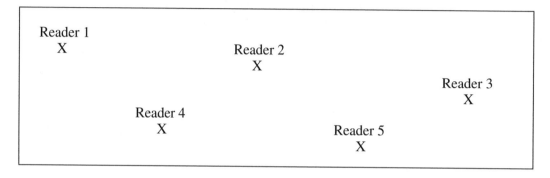

READER 1: On top of Old Smoky,
All covered with snow,
I lost my true lover,
By courting too slow.

READER 2: While courting is pleasure,
And parting is grief,
A false-hearted lover
Is worse than a thief.

READER 3: A thief they will rob you,
And take what you have,
But a false-hearted lover
Will take you to the grave.

READER 4: The grave will decay you,
Will turn you to dust.
Only one boy out of a hundred
A poor girl can trust.

READER 5: They'll tell you they love you,
To give your heart ease.
As soon as your back's turned,
They'll court who they please.

READER 1: 'Tis raining, 'tis hailing,
This dark stormy night.
Your horses can't travel,
For the moon gives no light.

READER 2: Go put up your horses,
And give them some hay.
Come sit down beside
As long as you can stay.

READER 3: My horses aren't hungry,
They won't eat your hay.
My wagon is loaded,
I'll feed on my way.

READER 4: As sure as the dew drops
Fall on the green corn,
Last night he was with me,
Tonight he is gone.

READER 5: I'll go back to Old Smoky,
To the mountains so high,
Where the wild birds and turtledoves
Can hear my sad cry.

ALL: Way down on Old Smoky,
All covered with snow,
I lost my true lover,
By courting too slow.

Home on the Range

STAGING: Each of the readers may be behind a music stand or lectern. The chorus may consist of anywhere from two to four readers. As an alternate option, you may wish to have the audience sing the chorus each time it comes up.

```
Chorus
X    X
X    X
              Reader 1              Reader 2              Reader 3
                 X                     X                     X
```

READER 1: Oh give me a home, where the buffalo roam,
Where the deer and the antelope play.
Where seldom is heard a discouraging word,
And the skies are not cloudy all day.

CHORUS: Home, home on the range,
Where the deer and the antelope play.
Where seldom is heard a discouraging word,
And the skies are not cloudy all day.

READER 2: Where the air is so pure, the zephyrs so free,
The breezes so balmy and light,
That I would not exchange my home on the range
For all the cities so bright.

CHORUS: Home, home on the range,
Where the deer and the antelope play.
Where seldom is heard a discouraging word,
And the skies are not cloudy all day.

READER 3: The red man was pressed from this part of the West,
He's likely no more to return
To the banks of the Red River, where seldom if ever,
Their flickering campfires burn.

CHORUS: Home, home on the range,
Where the deer and the antelope play.
Where seldom is heard a discouraging word,
And the skies are not cloudy all day.

From *American Folklore, Legends, and Tall Tales for Readers Theatre* by Anthony D. Fredericks. Westport, CT: Teacher Ideas Press. Copyright © 2008.

READER 1: How often at night when the heavens are bright
With the light of the glittering stars,
Have I stood here amazed and asked as I gazed,
If their glory exceeds that of ours.

CHORUS: Home, home on the range,
Where the deer and the antelope play.
Where seldom is heard a discouraging word,
And the skies are not cloudy all day.

READER 2: Oh, I love these wild flowers in this dear land of ours;
The curlew I love to hear scream.
And I love the white rocks and the antelope flocks
That graze on the mountain-tops green.

CHORUS: Home, home on the range,
Where the deer and the antelope play.
Where seldom is heard a discouraging word,
And the skies are not cloudy all day.

READER 3: Oh, give me a land where the bright diamond sand
Flows leisurely down the stream;
Where the graceful white swan goes gliding along,
Like a maid in a heavenly dream.

CHORUS: Home, home on the range,
Where the deer and the antelope play.
Where seldom is heard a discouraging word,
And the skies are not cloudy all day.

ALL READERS: Then I would not exchange my home on the range,
Where the dear and the antelope play.
Where seldom is heard a discouraging word,
And the skies are not cloudy all day.

CHORUS: Home, home on the range,
Where the deer and the antelope play.
Where seldom is heard a discouraging word,
And the skies are not cloudy all day.

Buffalo Gals

STAGING: Each reader should be standing, with a script in his or her hands. The chorus (which can consist of anywhere from two to five individuals) may be seated on tall stools or chairs throughout the performance.

```
                                                              Chorus
                                                              X   X   X
                                                                X   X
         Reader 1              Reader 2              Reader 3
            X                     X                     X
```

READER 1: As I was walking down the street,

READER 2: Down the street, down the street,

READER 1: A pretty gal I chanced to meet,

READER 3: Under the silvery moon.

CHORUS: Buffalo gals, won't you come out tonight,
Come out tonight, come out tonight.
Buffalo gals, won't you come out tonight,
And dance by the light of the moon.

READER 2: I asked her if she'd stop and talk,

READER 3: Stop and talk, stop and talk.

READER 2: Her feet covered up the whole sidewalk.

READER 1: She was fair to view.

CHORUS: Buffalo gals, won't you come out tonight,
Come out tonight, come out tonight.
Buffalo gals, won't you come out tonight,
And dance by the light of the moon.

READER 3: I asked her if she'd be my wife,

READER 1: Be my wife, be my wife.

READER 3: Then I'd be happy all my life,

READER 2: If she'd marry me.

CHORUS: Buffalo gals, won't you come out tonight,
Come out tonight, come out tonight.
Buffalo gals, won't you come out tonight,
And dance by the light of the moon.

READER 1: As I was walking down the street,

READER 2: Down the street, down the street,

READER 1: A pretty gal I chanced to meet,

READER 3: Under the silvery moon.

CHORUS: Buffalo gals, won't you come out tonight,
Come out tonight, come out tonight.
Buffalo gals, won't you come out tonight,
And dance by the light of the moon.

READER 2: I asked her if she'd stop and talk,

READER 3: Stop and talk, stop and talk.

READER 2: Her feet covered up the whole sidewalk.

READER 1: She was fair to view.

CHORUS: Buffalo gals, won't you come out tonight,
Come out tonight, come out tonight.
Buffalo gals, won't you come out tonight,
And dance by the light of the moon.

READER 3: I asked her if she'd be my wife,

READER 1: Be my wife, be my wife.

READER 3: Then I'd be happy all my life,

READER 2: If she'd marry me.

CHORUS: Buffalo gals, won't you come out tonight,
Come out tonight, come out tonight.
Buffalo gals, won't you come out tonight,
And dance by the light of the moon.

The Cowboy's Lament

STAGING: The four narrators should all be standing in a row across the staging area. Each may have a music stand to hold his or her script. You may wish to play some somber music softly in the background as this song is read to the audience. Obtain a recording of the song and share it with students after the presentation. (Artists who have recorded this song include Johnny Cash, Joan Baez, Roy Rogers, Marty Robbins, Chet Atkins, and Arlo Guthrie.) (A humorous and significantly modified version was done by the Smothers Brothers.)

Narrator 1	Narrator 2	Narrator 3	Narrator 4
X	X	X	X

NARRATOR 1: As I walked out in the streets of Laredo,
As I walked out in Laredo one day,
I spied a poor cowboy wrapped up in white linen,
Wrapped up in white linen as cold as the clay.

NARRATOR 2: Oh, beat the drum slowly and play the fife lowly,
Play the dead march as you carry me along.
Take me to the green valley, there lay the sod o'er me,
For I'm a young cowboy and I know I've done wrong.

NARRATOR 3: I see by your outfit that you are a cowboy—
These words he did say as I boldly stepped by:
Come sit down beside me and hear my sad story;
I am shot in the breast, and I know I must die.

NARRATOR 4: Let 16 gamblers come handle my coffin;
Let 16 cowboys come sing me a song.
Take me to the graveyard and lay the sod o'er me,
For I'm a poor cowboy, and I know I've done wrong.

NARRATOR 1: My friends and relations they live in the Nation;
They know not where their boy has gone.
He first came to Texas and hired to a ranchman.
Oh, I'm a young cowboy, and I know I've done wrong.

NARRATOR 2: It was once in the saddle I used to go dashing;
It was once in the saddle I used to go gay;
First to the dram-house and then to the card-house;
Got shot in the breast, and I am dying today.

NARRATOR 3: Get six jolly cowboys to carry my coffin.

NARRATOR 4: Get six pretty maidens to bear up my pall.
Put bunches of roses all over my coffin;
Put roses to deaden the sods as they fall.

NARRATOR 1: Then swing your rope slowly and rattle your spurs lowly,
And give a wild whoop as you carry me along.
And in the grave throw me and roll the sod o'er me,
For I'm a young cowboy, and I know I've done wrong.

NARRATOR 2: Oh, bury beside me my knife and my six-shooter,
My spurs on my heel, my rifle by my side.
And over my coffin put a bottle of brandy
That the cowboys may drink as they carry me along.

NARRATOR 3: Go bring me a cup, a cup of cold water,
To cool my parched lips, the cowboy then said.
Before I returned his soul had departed,
And gone to the round-up—the cowboy was dead.

NARRATOR 4: We beat the drum slowly and played the fife lowly,
And bitterly wept as we bore him along.
For we all loved our comrade, so brave, young, and handsome,
We all loved our comrade although he'd done wrong.

ALL: We all loved our comrade although he'd done wrong.

References

Cunningham, P., and R. Allington. 2003. *Classrooms That Work: They Can All Read and Write.* Boston: Allyn & Bacon.

Dixon, N., A. Davies, and C. Politano. 1996. *Learning with Readers Theatre: Building Connections.* Winnipeg, MB: Peguis Publishers.

Fredericks, A.D. 1993. *Frantic Frogs and Other Frankly Fractured Folktales for Readers Theatre.* Westport, CT: Teacher Ideas Press.

———. 2001. *Guided Reading for Grades 3–6.* Austin, TX: Harcourt Achieve.

———. 2007. *Nonfiction Readers Theatre for Beginning Readers.* Westport, CT: Teacher Ideas Press.

———. 2008a. *MORE Frantic Frogs and Other Frankly Fractured Folktales for Readers Theatre.* Westport, CT: Teacher Ideas Press.

———. 2008b. *African Legends, Myths, and Folktales for Readers Theatre.* Westport, CT: Teacher Ideas Press.

Martinez, M., N. Roser, and S. Strecker. 1999. " 'I Never Thought I Could Be a Star': A Readers Theatre Ticket to Reading Fluency." *The Reading Teacher* 52: 326–34.

Meinbach, A. M., A. D. Fredericks, and L. Rothlein. 2000. *The Complete Guide to Thematic Units: Creating the Integrated Curriculum.* Norwood, MA: Christopher-Gordon Publishers.

Rasinski, T. V. 2003. *The Fluent Reader: Oral Reading Strategies for Building Word Recognition, Fluency, and Comprehension.* New York: Scholastic.

Strecker, S. K., N. L. Roser, and M. G. Martinez. 1999. "Toward Understanding Oral Reading Fluency." *Yearbook of the National Reading Conference* 48: 295–310.

Tyler, B., and D. J. Chard. 2000. "Using Readers Theatre to Foster Fluency in Struggling Readers: A Twist on the Repeated Reading Strategy." *Reading and Writing Quarterly* 16: 163–8.

Wiggens, G., and J. McTighe. 1998. *Understanding by Design.* Alexandria, VA: Association for Supervision and Curriculum Development.

Wiske, M. S., ed. 1998. *Teaching for Understanding.* San Francisco: Jossey-Bass.

Wolf, S. 1998. "The Flight of Reading: Shifts in Instruction, Orchestration, and Attitudes Through Classroom Theatre." *Reading Research Quarterly* 33: 382–415.

More Teacher Resources

by

Anthony D. Fredericks

The following books are available from Teacher Ideas Press (88 Post Road West, Westport, CT 06881); 1-800-225-5800; http://www.teacherideaspress.com.

African Legends, Myths, and Folktales for Readers Theatre. ISBN 978-1-59158-633-3. (166pp.; $25.00).

> Teachers are continually looking for materials that will enhance the study of cultures around the world. This collection of readers theatre scripts offers just that through an approach to the cultural study of Africa that will be fun and motivational for students—and improve their reading fluency.

Building Fluency with Readers Theatre: Motivational Strategies, Successful Lessons and Dynamic Scripts to Develop Fluency, Comprehension, Writing and Vocabulary. ISBN 978- 1-59158-733-0. (234pp.; $35.00).

> Packed with practical ideas and loads of creative strategies, this resource offers teachers and librarians a wealth of innovative and dynamic techniques to stimulate and support the teaching of reading fluency across the elementary curriculum. This book is filled with the latest information, up-to-date data, and lots of inventive scripts for any classroom or library.

Frantic Frogs and Other Frankly Fractured Folktales for Readers Theatre. ISBN 1-56308-174-1 (124pp.; $19.50).

> Have you heard "Don't Kiss Sleeping Beauty, She's Got Really Bad Breath" or "The Brussels Sprouts Man (The Gingerbread Man's Unbelievably Strange Cousin)"? This resource (grades 4–8) offers 30 reproducible satirical scripts for rip-roaring dramatics in any classroom or library.

The Integrated Curriculum: Books for Reluctant Readers, Grades 2-5 (2nd Edition). ISBN 0-87287-994-1. (220pp.; $22.50).

> This book presents guidelines for motivating and using literature with reluctant readers. The book contains more than 40 book units on titles carefully selected to motivate the most reluctant readers.

Investigating Natural Disasters Through Children's Literature: An Integrated Approach. ISBN 1-56308-861-4. (194pp.; $28.00).

> Tap into students' inherent awe of storms, volcanic eruptions, hurricanes, earthquakes, tornadoes, floods, avalanches, landslides, and tsunamis to open their minds to the wonders and power of the natural world.

Involving Parents Through Children's Literature: P–K. ISBN 1-56308-022-2. (86pp.; $15.00).

Involving Parents Through Children's Literature: Grades 1–2. ISBN 1-56308-012-5. (96pp.; $14.50).

Involving Parents Through Children's Literature: Grades 3–4. ISBN 1-56308-013-3. (96pp.; $15.50).

Involving Parents Through Children's Literature: Grades 5–6. ISBN 1-56308-014-1. (108pp.; $16.00).

> This series of four books offers engaging activities for adults and children that stimulate comprehension and promote reading enjoyment. Reproducible activity sheets based on high-quality children's books are designed in a convenient format so that children can take them home.

The Librarian's Complete Guide to Involving Parents Through Children's Literature: Grades K–6. ISBN 1-56308-538-0. (138pp.; $24.50).

> Activities for 101 children's books are presented in a reproducible format, so librarians can distribute them to students to take home and share with parents.

MORE Frantic Frogs and Other Frankly Fractured Folktales for Readers Theatre. ISBN 978-1-59158-628-9. (166pp.; $25.00).

> Remember all the fun you had with the original *Frantic Frogs*? Well, they're back!! Here's another laugh-fest overflowing with scripts that will leave students (and teachers) rolling in the aisles (Don't miss "The Original Hip-Hop [by Busta Frog]") .

MORE Science Adventures with Children's Literature: Reading Comprehension and Inquiry-Based Science. ISBN 978-1-59158-619-7. (444pp.; $35.00).

> Get ready for hundreds of hands-on, minds-on projects that will actively engage students in positive learning experiences. Each of the 62 units offers book summaries, science topic areas, critical thinking questions, classroom resources, reproducible pages, and lots of easy-to-do activities, including science experiments for every grade level.

More Social Studies Through Children's Literature: An Integrated Approach. ISBN 1-56308-761-8. (226pp.; $27.50).

> Energize your social studies curriculum with dynamic, hands-on, minds-on projects based on such great children's books as *Amazing Grace*, *Fly Away Home*, and *Lon Po Po*. This book is filled with an array of activities and projects sure to "energize" any social studies curriculum.

Mother Goose Readers Theatre for Beginning Readers. ISBN 978-1-59158-500-8. (168pp.; $25.00).

> Designed especially for educators in the primary grades, this resource provides engaging opportunities that capitalize on children's enjoyment of Mother Goose rhymes. There is lots to share and lots to enjoy in the pages of this resource.

Much More Social Studies Through Children's Literature: A Collaborative Approach. ISBN 978-1-59158-445-2. (278pp.; $35.00).

This collection of dynamic literature-based activities will help any teacher or librarian energize the entire social studies curriculum and implement national (and state) standards. This resource is filled with hundreds of hands-on, minds-on projects.

Nonfiction Readers Theatre for Beginning Readers. ISBN 978-1-59158-499-5. (220pp.; $25.00).

This collection of science and social studies nonfiction scripts for beginning readers is sure to "jazz up" any language arts program in grades 1–3. Teachers and librarians will discover a wealth of creative opportunities to enhance fluency, comprehension, and appreciate of nonfiction literature.

Readers Theatre for American History. ISBN 1-56308-860-6. (174pp.; $30.00).

This book offers a participatory approach to American history in which students become active in several historical events. These 24 scripts give students a "you are there" perspective on critical milestones and colorful moments that have shaped the American experience.

Science Adventures with Children's Literature: A Thematic Approach. ISBN 1-56308-417-1. (190pp.; $24.50).

Focusing on the National Science Education Standards, this activity-centered resource uses a wide variety of children's literature to integrate science across the elementary curriculum. With a thematic approach, it features the best in science trade books along with stimulating hands-on, minds on activities in all the sciences.

Science Discoveries on the Net: An Integrated Approach. ISBN 1-56308-823-1. (316pp.; $27.50).

This book is designed to help teachers integrate the Internet into their science programs and enhance the scientific discoveries of students. The 88 units emphasize key concepts—based on national and state standards—throughout the science curriculum.

Silly Salamanders and Other Slightly Stupid Stuff for Readers Theatre. ISBN 1-56308-825-8. (162pp.; $23.50).

The third entry in the "wild and wacky" readers theatre trilogy is just as crazy and just as weird as the first two. This unbelievable resource offers students in grades 3–6 dozens of silly send-ups of well-known fairy tales, legends, and original stories.

Social Studies Discoveries on the Net: An Integrated Approach. ISBN 1-56308-824-X. (276pp.; $26.00).

This book is designed to help teachers integrate the Internet into their social studies programs and enhance the classroom discoveries of students. The 75 units emphasize key concepts —based on national and state standards—throughout the social studies curriculum.

Social Studies Through Children's Literature: An Integrated Approach. ISBN 1-87287-970-4. (192pp.; $24.00).

Each of the 32 instructional units contained in this resource utilizes an activity-centered approach to elementary social studies, featuring children's picture books such as *Ox-Cart Man, In Coal Country,* and *Jambo Means Hello.*

Songs and Rhymes Readers Theatre for Beginning Readers. ISBN 978-1-59158-627-2. (154pp.; $25.00).

Bring music, song, and dance into your classroom language arts curriculum with this delightful collection of popular rhymes and ditties. Beginning readers will enjoy learning about familiar characters in this engaging collection of scripts.

Tadpole Tales and Other Totally Terrific Titles for Readers Theatre. ISBN 1-56308-547-X. (116pp.; $18.50).

A follow-up volume to the best selling *Frantic Frogs and Other Frankly Fractured Folktales for Readers Theatre*, this book provides primary level readers (grades 1–4) with a humorous assortment of wacky tales based on well-known Mother Goose rhymes. More than 30 scripts and dozens of extensions will keep students rolling in the aisles.

Index

About the Author

Anthony D. Fredericks (afredericks60@comcast.net). Tony's background includes more than 38 years of experience as a classroom teacher, reading specialist, curriculum coordinator, staff developer, professional storyteller, and college professor. He is a prolific author, having written more than 70 teacher resource books, including the enormously popular *More Frantic Frogs and Other Frankly Fractured Folktales for Readers Theatre*, the best-selling *Building Fluency with Readers Theatre*, the celebrated *Much More Social Studies Through Children's Literature*, and the dynamic *Readers Theatre for American History*.

In addition, he's authored more than three dozen award-winning children's books, including *The Tsunami Quilt: Grandfather's Story, Near One Cattail: Turtles, Logs and Leaping Frogs, Animal Sharpshooters*, and *A Is for Anaconda: A Rainforest Alphabet Book*.

Tony currently teaches elementary methods courses in reading, language arts, science, social studies, and children's literature at York College in York, Pennsylvania. In addition, he is a popular and enthusiastic visiting children's author to elementary schools throughout North America, where he celebrates books, writing, and storytelling.